EUROPE IN COLOR

Europe

IN COLOR

BY THE EDITORS OF

HOLIDAY

Published by The Curtis Publishing Company, Philadelphia

Distributed by Doubleday & Company, Inc., Garden City, N.Y.

Frontispiece—The Louvre in Paris. One of the great art monuments of the world, it has a long and turbulent history—fortress, dungeon, pleasure palace, site of burnings and massacres. Today its endless halls and sunny gardens are places of repose and artistic contemplation.

CONTENTS

THE MEANING OF EUROPE *by Allan Nevins* . . . 6

FAVORITE TOURS 11

ENGLAND 15

IRELAND 43

SCANDINAVIA 53

THE LOW COUNTRIES 65

CENTRAL EUROPE 75

THE IBERIAN PENINSULA 123

THE MEDITERRANEAN 145

PHOTO CREDITS 191

INDEX 192

The Meaning of Europe

by Allan Nevins

BRITAIN

"Everybody was going to Europe," wrote Mark Twain, in 1867. Today, nearly everybody is still going to Europe. Schoolteachers who have scrimped for long months to see Stratford and Notre Dame are buying tourist-class tickets. Bankers and movie magnates are booking first-class passage to Paris and the Riviera. Businessmen and diplomats are jamming the airplanes. Publishers and writers are going to England, designers and artists to France, mountain climbers to Switzerland, archaeologists to Greece, and students everywhere. People are going for a thousand different reasons.

What is the lure of Europe? Nostalgia, thirst for culture, a wish to compare civilizations, escapism—"Out of my country and myself I go," as a poet sings—a hope for adventure: all these elements impel people to travel. But a more fundamental force is also discernible: American life is fixed between two poles—the old European homeland and the rugged frontier; and, in some degree, every one of us feels the tug of these two poles.

This is a healthy fact for American life, for Europe and America correct and supplement each other. Sometimes the pull of rival forces—the polite, artistic, mature civilization of Europe, with all its lessons from the past, and the strenuous, self-reliant temper of the West, with all its ambitions for the future—divides members of the same family. Henry Adams, for example, went as a young man to England, imbibed the best essence of London and Paris, and to the end of his days remained thoroughly Europeanized. His brother, Charles Francis Adams, Jr., fought in the Civil War, took up railroading, became president of the Union Pacific, and knew more about Western

ways than most Coloradans. Many Americans, however, have responded to both polar attractions and have acquired the finest gifts of both East and West.

We are all spiritual children of Europe; and nearly all of us are also children by blood tie, near or remote. Some sense of family descent lurks in our hearts, whether we look back to Plymouth Rock or to Ellis Island. Many thousands of American doughboys in the two world wars took European brides, and have been busy rearing children with European grandparents. Even Americans of the so-called newer immigration, who usually have a less lively consciousness of the link with the homeland than the older stocks, have sometimes kept or regained this sense. Many of them cannot forget Europe and wish to see if the river, the castle, the village dances, the songs are what their parents or grandparents said they were.

The blood tie of the older stock has seemed the stronger because of the close affinity between American civilization and that of Western Europe. The Germans who "fought mit Sigel" never forgot the Rhine, the Irishmen who voted for Al Smith never forgot the Shannon. Blood is thicker than water, said Com. Josiah Tattnall when, as flag officer on the Eastern station, he joined the British tars in fighting the Chinese; and though the sentiment sounds ridiculous in after-dinner speeches ("treacle is thicker still," growled Lord Lee of Fareham), still sentiment sometimes gets its hour. The two Roosevelts always remembered their Dutch strain. That other great American, Mr. Dooley, softened his satire when he talked about a family reunion of the Roscommon Dooleys, so much superior to the Fermanagh Dooleys. "Some iv us hadn't spoke frindly to each other f'r twenty years, an' we set aroun' and tol' stories iv Roscommon an' its green fields, an' the stirabout

pot that was niver filled, an' the blue sky over-
head, an' the boggy ground undherfoot.''

We might say that the British stock is less in-
clined to think of its blood ties with Europe than
the Germans, Irish, or Huguenots; partly because
it has been here so long, has given the country so
many British institutions, and takes the subject so
much for granted. Down to 1776, Britain and the
American colonies had the same history. Yet
many a Yankee, too, feels his pulse quicken when
he first sights the chalk cliffs.

As generations pass, Americans unescapably
become a more mixed people, the blood of dozens
of national stocks mingling indistinguishably; and
the memory of far-off origins inevitably becomes
dim. But other ties than blood, fortunately, have
an increasing strength. Above all else, the lure of
Europe lies in the grandeur of her cultural heritage; a heritage we share, and against which we
measure our own performances.

For nearly all our culture, including the con-
summate culture of democracy, was born and developed in Europe and came to us from there. Our
law came from Rome, the Roman Senate and
Forum. Our architecture came from Greece, and
from Rome, and from Normandy, and from the
English country house. Our language came from
Germany, France and England, with liberal
pepper-and-salting from Scandinavia, Italy, and
Spain. Our art, from Leonardo da Vinci to Picasso,

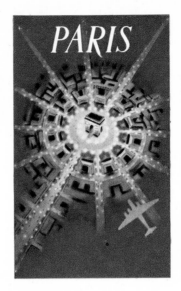

has deep roots in Europe. Our literature goes back
to beloved English writers. Our music—Messrs.
Bach, Beethoven and Brahms—comes to us from
overseas. Our theater, direct descendant from
Shakespeare and Ben Jonson, is again a European
heritage. And even the delights of our table, our
food and our wine, have been influenced and still are
influenced by the gastronomic culture of Europe.

Europe may be impoverished by wars, down at
the heels, racked by anxieties for the future, hardly
able in some countries to maintain stable democratic governments; still the glories of its letters
and art shine as resplendent as ever. We no longer
think that the older nations conspire to under-
value us, nor do we complain, as Lowell did, of a
certain condescension in foreigners. The shoe is
on the other foot. They accuse *us* of condescension. But the American still acknowledges their
transcendent achievement in literature, painting,
sculpture, music and architecture. Where we have
produced great talent, Europe has produced high
genius.

The mere sight-seer, wandering through streets
and museums with a Baedeker in hand, obtains a
superficial (and sometimes irritated) impression
of all this culture. Usually he is impressed. Sometimes, if he is not well schooled, he deems the
glories of Edinburgh, Paris, and Rome over-
praised. He may react like the young Mark Twain
of *Innocents Abroad*, the exuberant, iconoclastic
wag from Hannibal and Virginia City who left a

7

trail of cheap jocosities and boastful comparisons as he wandered through France and Italy. But like many jaded tourists, Mark learned more than he supposed. He poked deprecatory fun at his education in the field of sacred painting. "We have seen thirteen thousand St. Jeromes, and twenty-two thousand St. Marks, and sixteen thousand St. Matthews." In reality, he was forming a basis for the realistic appreciation of art. And even then he was moved to enthusiasm by the palace of Versailles, the cathedral of Milan, and the statue of the Dying Gladiator.

As anyone can see by looking at a little of our history, the lodestone of European culture has made itself felt in much more efficient ways than through Baedeker, the night clubs of Montmartre, and hop-skip-jump tours (very well for a beginning) of London, Paris, the Rhine and the Alps.

Provincialism is a great enemy of true culture. It makes the Dane less provincial to look around Germany, and the Frenchman less provincial to have a run through Italy. William Hazlitt tells how an English sculptor came back from Rome, where he had inspected the work of Michelangelo and Cellini; went to review his own pieces in Westminster Abbey; and exclaimed in despair, "My God, they look like tobacco pipes!" Americans are specially prone to provincialism. Our public schools give most young people the impression that the United States has been right in every quarrel, and is better off than other countries in practically every way.

A trip abroad is good for the soul because it quickly shakes these limited views. The American tourist finds that Bern, in Switzerland, and Cardiff, in Wales, are better planned than any American city of their size. He discovers that the English and West Germans buy more books per capita than we do. He finds out that an English schoolboy is usually a year ahead of the American schoolboy of the same age, and that an Oxford man is generally better educated in three years than an American university man in four. He soon learns that if American broadcasting has something to teach the British in liveliness, British broadcasting has much more to teach us in taste and substance. He discovers that by European standards New York and Chicago are

intolerably dirty, and quickly perceives in great parts of Europe a natural artistic sense quite lacking in most of his own country.

As Americans go abroad for formal learning, and for a view of standards that will make them less provincial, so they go to Europe to see places, buildings, and ruins associated with history and literature. Beyond question, the most profitable travel is given interest by wide reading and vitality by a lively imagination. The best way to see Britain's Lake Country is with a volume of Wordsworth in one's pocket; the visitor is less interested in the London of today than in Dickens's London—the Soho of Doctor Manette, the Adelphi Terrace of David Copperfield, the White Hart Inn where Pickwick met Sam Weller, the Marshalsea Prison of Little Dorrit, and the other storied spots, including the Baker Street of Sherlock Holmes. Thackeray's London and Balzac's Paris are almost equally seductive; and then the Scott country, the Hardy country, the Bronte country, Flaubert's Normandy, and all the rest.

Imagination is above everything else indispensable. The tourist who drives along the highroad between Winchester and Salisbury passes the remains of an old Roman encampment, with its double lines of ramparts. To the uninitiated they are just grassy embankments. But if the traveler has read Caesar's *Commentaries*, he sees at once that they fit the descriptions in that classic text. And if he possesses a fertile imagination, he sees Caesar himself, his bald head burned red by the midsummer sun of Southern England, striding about with the short Roman sword in hand; or he watches the close-embodied ranks of a legion cresting the nearest hill. Claude G. Bowers, the historian and diplomatist, has told how he and his daughter, flushed with excitement, followed the very route from Versailles to Paris which Marie Antoinette was forced to take in 1789; their imaginations painted the hooting mob, the frightened king and the sobbing queen.

It is because of its historical and literary associations that Europe has always had a special appeal to American artists, poets, and novelists. The immense variety of life between Dublin and Warsaw, the centuries of crowded events have made the continent a rich quarry of materials. How, indeed, can any field of art divorce itself from European inspiration? It will be a bleak day when Montmartre and Florence are not crowded with American artists, as Leipzig and Munich are now bleak without groups of our music students.

Learning, standards, history, art: what else lies in the European lodestone? If we stopped with these, we would omit one of the largest elements—ideas. Here Americans *must* turn to Europe, with its twenty diverse peoples, its fewer materialistic tasks and preoccupations, its long tradition of the mind. For Europe has lived more intellectually than America; ever since the Enlightenment and the French Revolution, men overseas have thought more radically (in the good sense of the word) than in our busier, more prosperous, more homogeneous land.

To certain types of Americans, ideas afford a headier stimulation than anything else, and the diversity of European ideas has always been a powerful magnet. Tyrannies rose and fell; the ideas went on. Robert Owen, Louis Blanc and Karl Marx held the Socialist banner aloft. Darwin and Herbert Spencer made evolution a regenerating force. Galton, Bergson, Freud, Tolstoy—what mighty trains of ideas each brought in and what enthusiasm many Americans felt in adopting them! Ruskin, William Morris, Shaw and H. G. Wells all had their schemes for remaking human society. Yesterday, existentialism held the stage; today, newer ideas are seizing men's minds.

While ideas are readily exportable, Americans have always manifested a lively interest in seeking them at the fountainhead. Tom Paine simply had to fling himself into the French Revolution, and Charles A. Dana reveled amid the uprisings of 1848. When evolution dawned, the great historian John Fiske rushed across the Atlantic to greet all

Hospitable
GERMANY

the leaders of the new faith. Only yesterday, Gertrude Stein was in Paris, steeping herself in the ideas of the rising French artists, and a dozen young American writers were dogging the footsteps of James Joyce to learn his literary principles.

Out of the clash of ideas, some wrong, some right, comes illumination. As America grows in power, the movement of ideas becomes more a two-way traffic than of old; but if Europeans now have to turn west, Americans still have to turn east.

And a higher kind of inspiration than any we have yet named comes from the constant rediscovery of Europe. This is the spiritual impulse which is the most important part of the stream of Occidental civilization.

Great are matters of the mind, but greater still are such values as liberty, justice, equality, freedom of utterance, religious tolerance, and democracy. Europe, from the Agora in Athens to Runnymede on the Thames, is the land where most of

GREECE

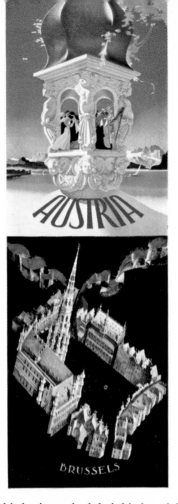

AUSTRIA

BRUSSELS

monument to Giordano Bruno on the spot where he was burned"—so runs the inscription. A bas relief shows him at his trial, uttering the proud words: "Perchance I hear this sentence with less fear than you pronounce it." Seeing that monument, no one can help thinking of the long battle for freedom of thought, belief and expression.

We have offered many reasons for going to Europe, for turning east; but one of the most important remains—to have a good time. Let us by all means go to Europe for refreshment, gaiety, and entertainment. With its restaurants and theaters, its fetes and exhibitions, and its endless alternations of scenery and manners, it offers them in full store. In fact, a trip to Europe demands fun, relaxation, a chance to savor all that is offered. We need not think too deliberately of our blood ties, of our share in European history, of the standards which will correct our provincialism, of our debt in letters, art, and ideas, and of our spiritual inheritance. These considerations will steal upon us while we are enjoying ourselves. If we have wit and vitality, we cannot travel about Europe without being reminded of such values at every turn.

For Europe has an unfailing magic; age cannot wither, nor custom stale, its infinite variety. The traveler sits looking at Capri lying like a fairy isle upon a sea with the soft bloom of grapes, the Vesuvian cone and the Sorrentine mountain in the background etherealized by distance. As the sun drops into the haze, the scene takes on the gorgeous hues of a landscape by Turner. Or the traveler sits dining at La Tour d'Argent, gazing at Notre Dame and the Seine, and thinking of the diverse throngs that have moved up and down the streets in the long centuries since Victor Hugo's Quasimodo made the cathedral his fortress. Or he stands on Trinity Bridge, over the Cam, its waters filled with punting couples. Before him stretches the august Gothic expanse of St. John's College; on the right is Wren's incomparable Library of Trinity, and the chapel with its statues of Newton, Macaulay, and Tennyson; to the left are the gardens and the splendid avenue of elms. The chimes of St. Mary's Church fall softly on his ear, precisely as Bacon and Milton heard them. In such places, we draw in the meaning of Europe with the very air we breathe.

these inestimable heritages had their birth and development; and the thoughtful traveler is impressed most of all by the reminders of these ancient principles and aspirations.

He will find these reminders in a thousand places and monuments, the chief glory of the elder nations. Poor indeed is the pilgrim who can stand before the Parthenon, or in the Sistine Chapel, or under the roof of the House of Commons, without feeling moved by the mighty forces which these sites represent. The visitor may gain a sudden revelation of the spiritual wealth of the past in less conspicuous spots. Perhaps it will come in viewing Thorwaldsen's wounded lion at Lucerne, emblem of the heroism of the Swiss Guard; in Paris, standing at Pasteur's tomb; in seeing the streets of Stratford thronged with visitors from every land on earth; or perhaps in London, gazing at the statue of Nurse Edith Cavell, with its unforgettable quotation, "Patriotism is not enough." There are European battlefields from Marston Moor to Marathon where the spirit of Liberty walks all but visibly. In Rome, modern Italy has lifted a statue to Giordano Bruno. "The country to which he looked forward raises this

Favorite Tours

Austria, The Italian Lakes, Switzerland

● Here, in a twelve-day package, are the mountains and lakes, castles and palaces of Austria, Switzerland and the Italian Lake region, a 1570-mile motor-coach tour.

You start with dinner and an overnight stay at the Hotel Touring in Basel, Switzerland; next morning, you head along the Rhine on the first lap of a three-day journey to Vienna. You pass through picturesque Laufenburg with its ruined castle overlooking the river rapids, thence to St. Gall, center for remarkable embroideries, laces and cotton products, where you see a Benedictine Abbey that was a great power in the Middle Ages. Your route follows Lake Constance (the Boden-See), huge reservoir of the Rhine and a natural barrier between Switzerland and Germany, to the Austrian border.

First stop in Austria is Feldkirch, a relic of the Middle Ages, with its cobbled streets, ancient house-fronts, and 700-year-old Schattenburg Castle "haunted" by a knightly ghost. The road then climbs steeply to the beautiful high Arlberg region, a lonely, wild, mountainous country slashed by thousands of rushing glacial streams. St. Anton, the principal town in the Arlberg, is remarkable for its lovely mountain-chalet architecture. Austrian law requires all new building in the Arlberg to follow the regional style, and St. Anton looks like a stage-set for a Tyrolean operetta. You drive on through the Tyrol and a succession of Alpine villages with wide-eaved, white-faced houses, all flower-laden in season.

You stay overnight in Innsbruck and sample fine Tyrolean wines and cheeses. In the little cobbled Stadtplatz is the Golden Dachl, a small, Gothic, balconied building with a gilded roof and gay carvings of strolling players.

Next day, still in the Tyrol, you cut across an arm of Germany to Berchtesgaden, Hitler's famous mountain retreat, then recross into Austria. You go through Salzburg (you'll have a return visit) to St. Wolfgang in the lake country, a charming resort town. After a night in St. Wolfgang, you reach Vienna via the high-altitude spa of Bad Ischl and Linz.

In a day and a half in Vienna, take in particularly the recently reconstructed Opera, now more magnificent than ever after its gutting in the war; the beautiful circle of avenues that make up the Ringstrasse; the Gothic beauty of refurbished St. Stephen's Cathedral; the famous wrought-iron Michaeler Gate and Hofburg Palace; beautiful Schoenbrunn Palace, the only palace in Europe still decorated as it was when its imperial tenants left it. And, of course, no evening in Vienna is complete without a visit to a wine-garden or a deep, cellar café.

After lunch on the sixth day you go back to Salzburg and stay overnight. One of the world's loveliest cities, Salzburg plays host to the music world at its festival during late July and August, and there are open-air theatrical performances in the dramatic cathedral square.

You turn south now to climb one of the most dramatic mountain highways in the world, the breath-taking Grossglockner High Alpine road. At one point, you can drink beer on a terrace that commands a view of the mountains, forests and lakes of four countries: Austria, Germany, Italy and Switzerland. Swinging down, you enter Heiligenblut, perched among towering mountains. You spend the night in Lienz, dominated by its turreted, pastel castle in the main square.

Next morning, you cross the Italian Dolomites and the plains of Northern Italy to Venice. For a day and a half you absorb the colorful life of this water-borne masterpiece. On the Grand Canal you can glide in a gondola past magnificent palaces, churches and luxurious hotels; you have time to explore the quiet, narrow, watery byways, as well as the major attractions of St. Mark's Square, the Cathedral, Doge's Palace, Bridge of Sighs and Rialto.

On the tenth day, you're on to Padua, Vicenza, Verona and Sirmione, skirting thirty-two-mile-long Lake Garda, largest of the Italian lakes, and crossing the plains of Lombardy to Milan for the night. Take in Milan's great Duomo, second-largest church in the world, and visit the Galleria, with its glass-roofed arcades of shops.

Next day, you ride beside Lake Como and see Villa d'Este, the fabulous 16th Century villa set in endless formal gardens, thick with semitropical foliage, statues, fountains and cypress trees. After lunch at Menaggio you reach the Swiss border and the road climbs through high Alpine country to the Maloja Pass on the Engadine plateau. Then you run through a lofty twelve-mile valley to St. Moritz. The twin villages of St. Moritz-Dorf, on a terrace 200 feet above St. Moritz Lake, and St. Moritz-Bad, in the plain south of the lake, form one of Switzerland's most celebrated holiday resorts.

Your last day you cross the eastern Alps through the bleak Julier Pass to Chur, a town with charming medieval sections of narrow streets and picturesque overhanging buildings. You drop down then to skirt the Wallensee and Zurich See en route to Zurich, Switzerland's largest city, an immaculately clean place, with wide tree-lined streets. After lunch there you return through pastoral northern Switzerland to Basel, where your tour ends.

Linjebuss conducts this tour from June through September.

Spain's treasure cities, baroque cathedrals, ancient monasteries, dramatic paintings, and relics of Roman and Moorish domination are all brought together for you in a seventeen-day, 1744-mile motor-coach tour.

You start in the Basque country, at Irún on the French border, then drive to San Sebastián, on the Bay of Biscay, where the government, foreign representatives, gay crowds of social Spain come up from Madrid and set the place aglitter. You drive on and spend the night at Burgos, where next day you visit the fine 13th Century Gothic cathedral and the dazzling, sculptured royal tombs in the monastery Cartuja de Miraflores.

You take the twisting road to Madrid over mountain ranges and through the 4585-foot-high Somosierra Pass. You have three days in Madrid, with a sight-seeing tour the first day that takes in: the Prado Museum, Spain's greatest treasure house, containing priceless collections of Velasquez, Murillo, El Greco and Goya; Retiro Park, a 17th Century garden loaded with king-size statuary; modern Madrid and the entirely rebuilt University City.

The next two days you are on your own, to browse in Madrid, or visit nearby Toledo or El Escorial. Toledo still looks like the famous El Greco painting of it, and the house where El Greco lived and worked is a museum containing much of his work.

The great monastery-palace of El Escorial, thirty miles from Madrid, is in a barren, mountain-ringed plain. The severely Renaissance exterior gives no hint of the priceless tapestries, portraits, paintings, fabulously decorated living quarters of past kings and nobles of Spain within. Beneath the gigantic Greek- and Roman-styled church within the Escorial walls is the burial place of all the kings of Spain except three. The chamber is of black marble, with row upon row of marble sarcophagi all exactly alike.

Your sixth day, you head for Córdoba, traversing country associated with Don Quixote. On your seventh morning, in Córdoba, you see the curious *Mesquita*, a mosquelike cathedral built in the 8th Century by an Emir of the Caliph of Baghdad. Then you go to Seville for two nights and a day.

Seville is gay, bright with sun, flowers and semitropical foliage. You visit: the Museo de Bellas Artes, which houses the finest Murillos in Spain; the majestic cathedral and Giralda Tower; the Alcazar, former palace of Moorish and Spanish kings, with its exquisite columns, palms and flowering trees. You also tour the Triana quarter of the city, haunt of gypsies.

You move along now to Jerez de la Frontera, home of sherry; thence to the beautiful little port of Algeciras, where you can gaze across the bay at Gibraltar. You follow the delightful southern coast, the Spanish Riviera, to Malaga on its curving bay.

The eleventh day, you explore Malaga's ancient byways, its fountain courts, the ruins of the great *Alcazaba*, an 11th Century fortress. Then up into the mountains, for two days in Spain's jewel city—Granada. Here are mountain views, clear skies, luxuriant foliage, lovely old buildings, gardens and—the Alhambra. This delicate confection of courts,

Spain

halls and graceful rooms is the finest example of west-of-Islam architecture in Europe. From the Alhambra, you walk along a cypress-lined path to the lovely Generalife Gardens, a place of luxuriant, terraced slopes and murmurous fountains flowing down tile-lined aquaducts to calm reflecting pools. You also visit the tombs of Columbus's sponsors, Ferdinand and Isabella.

It's a two-day trip to Valencia, through orchards, orange groves, flower plantations and rice fields. High lights are: Murcia, with its 18th Century atmosphere; Alicante, where ships leave for the island paradises of Mallorca and Ibiza; and the beautiful village of Benidorm, founded by seaborne Greeks in the 8th Century B.C.

Valencia, where you spend two nights and a day, is a city of gaiety and fiestas. Its most notable buildings are the immense Gothic 15th Century Silk Exchange, with its magnificent star-vaulted roof and rows of twisted columns, and the Baroque 13th Century Cathedral.

Your last day takes you up the lovely Mediterranean coast to Tarragona, dramatically set on a hill overlooking the sea, and blessed with five great beaches. And your tour ends in Barcelona, Spain's most important commercial and industrial city, a majestic place that will probably tempt you to stay and see it on your own.

This tour is offered by the Autotransporte Turistico Español, S. A.

● The wild, misty beauty of Scotland's lakes, mountains, glens and heathery hillsides, ancient castles, the sense of history everywhere—these are the background of a six-day motor-coach tour from Edinburgh to Glasgow.

The roughly circular, 700-mile swing begins as you ride out Edinburgh's garden-bordered, castle-dominated Princes Street. You pass through Stirling, where an ancient castle, a favorite royal residence of the Stewarts, frowns down from a 340-foot bluff, then you cross the Forth River and get a distant view of the cone of Ben ("Mount") Lomond. Next come the Trossachs ("bristly country"), the setting of Scott's *Lady of the Lake*, which contain the charming little Loch Achray, set against towering Ben Venue. You go east then to Perth, skirting Loch Tay, celebrated for trout.

The second day's drive takes you first to Scone and its ancient Abbey from which the famous Coronation Stone was removed to London by Edward I in the 13th Century. Pastoral, green, rolling land flows upward, then gives way to rugged, wild mountain scenery. The road climbs through the Devil's Elbow, highest point attained by any main road in Britain (2200 feet), and you get a spectacular view across Highland mountains. Down to Braemar and thence to many-turreted Balmoral Castle. From May through July, the grounds are open to visitors if the royal family is not in residence. You move on, following the river Dee, rich in trout and salmon, to Aberdeen on the North Sea. This city of gray granite buildings is a seaport and fishing center (just the spot to try Scottish kippers and finnan haddie), with beaches, golf courses, and lovely Deeside country around it.

The third morning, you follow the river Don and, outside Inverurie, you enter desolate hills crowned with ruined castles and ancient forts. In Elgin you see a 13th Century cathedral ruin, then take a side trip to the seaside resort of Lossiemouth. You head for Inverness via Nairn, which is surrounded by such landmarks as Hardmuir (Macbeth's "blasted heath" and meeting place of the three witches), Cawdor Castle, and the battlefield of Culloden. Inverness occupies a beautiful site at the head of Inverness Firth and the northeast end of the Great Glen that contains Loch Ness.

On the fourth day you follow the shore of Loch Ness (watching, of course, for the monster) down the Great Glen to Fort William, take-off point for climbing Ben Nevis (4406 feet), highest mountain in Britain. You go through Glencoe, among the most magnificent glens in Scotland, reach Loch Awe, a twenty-five-mile-long lake studded with tree-tufted islands and surrounded by wooded mountains.

Your fifth day you can just look at Loch Awe, or optional excursions are available. Best is the steamer trip from Oban to the islands of Iona and Staffa. Three-mile-long Iona is the ancient burial place of Scottish kings and princes; Macbeth was the last monarch buried there, in 1057 (preceded by his murderee, Duncan, in 1040). It is also the place where Saint Columba established a mission in 563 A.D. and spread Christianity through Scotland. Off Staffa you'll see strange basaltic column formations and Fin-

The Scottish Highlands

SCOTLAND

Inverness
Elgin
Fort William
Aberdeen
Balmoral Castle
Oban
Perth
GLASGOW
EDINBURGH

gal's Cave, a great grotto with an opening that towers sixty feet above high-water mark.

On the last day of the tour, you skirt the rugged coast of Argyll, then turn up fiordlike Loch Fyne, a forty-two-mile arm of the sea. After a stop at the picturesque little town of Inveraray, you cross a narrow range of hills to Scotland's most celebrated lake, Loch Lomond. Your route curves down the loch's western side, bringing magnificent views of richly colored mountains and hills. Soon you are on the banks of the Clyde, and into Glasgow, Scotland's largest city. Here, in the towering shipyards which you pass, many of the world's greatest ocean liners were born. It is a city that invites browsing, too, with a great university (founded in 1451), a lovely cathedral, and an outstanding art gallery that includes Raphaels, Rembrandts and Titians.

The tour is operated by Thos. Cook & Son.

Paris to Nice

● Almost all Americans who visit France make a point of seeing Paris and the Riviera, but these are more cosmopolitan than French, and it is in between that the real France lies— the colorful regions of Île de France, Burgundy, the Alps of Savoie and

Dauphiné, and Provence. There is no better way of discovering this essential France than by motoring from Paris to Nice. You can do this best in your own or a rented car, but several bus lines cover the same terrain in two to two and one half days. Any French Government Tourist Office in main U. S. and European cities will direct you to them.

Leave Paris in the early morning, passing her huge airport at Orly and the magnificent 42,000-acre forest reserve of Fontainebleau with its lovely royal château. Then you cross the fertile plains of Brie into Sens, whose cathedral is one of the oldest Gothic structures and a model for England's Canterbury. At Auxerre, see the famous stained-glass cathedral windows that illustrate more than 350 Biblical and legendary subjects, and continue through quiet little Avallon, with its ancient buildings grouped about its Romanesque church. Saulieu, in Burgundy, is noted for its fine food and wine.

In Autun, stop to look over the traces of her Gallo-Roman glory: the ancient city gates, the remains of a Roman temple and theater and the fine Romanesque sculptures of the cathedral. If you break your journey overnight here, stay at the famous Hôtel St. Louis et Poste and try its *coq au vin* for dinner.

Take the road to Chalon-sur-Saône and follow the Saône River to Tournus and the abbey of l'An Mille, which shows influences of both Asia Minor and Carolingian Gaul. Go through Bourg-en-Bresse, Nantua and Saint-Julien-en-Genevois to Annecy, one of France's most beautiful lake resorts, an Alpine Venice with its buildings reflected in little canals that flow into the lake. Next is the famous spa of Aix-les-Bains, with a superb climate and equally wonderful mountain setting. Below Chambéry, you enter the scenic splendor

of La Grande Chartreuse, a region of fantastic mountains, bottomless gorges, wild forests, and the beautiful, austere monastery that was the birthplace of the renowned liqueur. At Col de Porte the road climbs to 4347 feet, then descends toward Grenoble, opening a magnificent view over Graisivaudan, one of France's most fertile valleys.

Mountain-encircled Grenoble, on the banks of the Isère, is the crowning jewel and most Parisian of all France's provincial cities. She is famed for her internationally flavored university, her museums and the lovely Place Grenette, bustling with cafés and market stalls. If you stay overnight in Grenoble, try the Hôtel des Trois Dauphins, and get acquainted with Dauphiné gastronomy at the restaurant Poularde Bressane, specializing in mountain trout and game dishes.

South of Grenoble, you cross the 17th Century arched bridge at Claix, and motor through Vercors and Trièves with mountains forming your horizon. You pass 6562-foot-high Needle Rock, first conquered in 1492—the first recorded scaling in the annals of mountain climbing. At Col de la Croix-Haute you cross an abrupt climatic boundary—from Alpine pastures and pine forests to Mediterranean vegetation. You drive through Sisteron, with its citadel perched on a rock rising from the river bed, then through the gorges of the Verdon and into Grasse, where France's perfume industry turns ten tons of flowers into two ounces of essence.

The road now crosses typical Provençal landscapes—tones of dusty pinks and grays accented by silvery olive groves and luxuriant greenery. Then it's the glittering arc of the Riviera; gay, sun-drenched Nice, tropical Juan-les-Pins with its sandy beach, Antibes and celebrity-studded Eden Roc.

ENGLAND

ENGLAND

At the Trooping of the Colour in front of the Horseguards Building,
Queen Elizabeth takes the salute on her horse, Winston. This brilliant
and colorful ceremony (*see also pages 24, 25*) is watched by other
members of the Royal Family from the windows above the Trooping ground.

17

England's lure to the traveler is almost too various to isolate. To the American it must always represent one of the richest and most constantly flowing sources of his national heritage, for our language, many of our institutions and customs have been borrowed wholesale from the British Isles.

England presents many vistas to charm almost every variety of traveler. Historically, its monuments are living records of the growth of civilization. These run from Stonehenge, whose original Druidic rites are still shrouded in mystery, to Westminster Abbey, the Houses of Parliament, the Tower of London and the Channel coast, where Drake crumpled an empire when his hardy seamen turned back the Spanish Armada. The bookman can find familiar scenes in the Lake Country beloved of Wordsworth, Leigh Hunt and Coleridge, in Chaucer's Canterbury, in Shakespeare's Stratford-upon-Avon, in the Cheshire Cheese, Bloomsbury and Tintern Abbey. Sportsmen find themselves at home on English golf links, fishing in British streams or shooting grouse. Pageantry continues to bloom in royal appearances, in the changing of the guard, even in the cut of the uniform of a bobby directing traffic. There is calm, clear beauty spread lavishly through the English countryside, quaintness without affectation in wayside inns and small villages, splendor in cathedrals and streamlined efficiency in modern British factories. Few countries have so many already implanted moods ready and waiting for the visitor, whether it be the London-fogged atmosphere of a Hitchcock movie, the turreted romance of Ivanhoe, or the merry, Lincoln-green free forest of Robin Hood.

England goes all out in tourist attractions. August, for example, sees such special events as the Musical and Floral Fete at Shrewsbury, the Southport Flower Show, International Athletic Meetings at London, and, if you want really to get into the swim of English enthusiasm, attend one of the many cricket matches in London. Other celebrations that continue through August include the Regency Exhibition at Brighton and of course the famous Edinburgh Festival. The Royal National Eisteddfod, a gathering of the bards, is held in Wales during the early part of August.

England's traditions, fortunately, include making visitors happy. Hotels and inns in graduated price ranges are conveniently located. Railways crisscross the island and there are car-rental arrangements for those who like to strike out for themselves off the beaten path. Theater, sports, music and pure and simple sight-seeing are available in abundance. England offers all the excitement of discovery with the added surprise of rediscovery of a common past.

A London Royal Horse Guards trooper wears full ceremonial dress. *At right* are the famous Beefeaters. These Yeoman Warders, nicknamed for the hearty rations of beef they drew at court, are a most magnificent reminder of Shakespeare's London. They pose here in state splendour by the Tower of London.

This delightful pastoral view from the lake shore in St. James Park,
London, shows the romantic pinnacles of Whitehall, seat of government,
in the distance. *At left*, an unusual metropolitan view from
one of London's fire towers pictures the great dome of St. Paul's.

London's heartbeat quickens with pure British pride when the Trooping
of the Colour celebrates the birthday of the Queen. (*See next two pages.*)

The House of Commons Chamber, plain and austere, is where the real business of Britain's lawmaking is battled out. Members of the party in power sit on the right, the Loyal Opposition on the left. *At right* is the richly elaborate House of Lords, meeting place of Britain's nobility. It is longer by twelve feet to accommodate the Throne which can be seen at the far end.

Claridge's Hotel in London is the scene of frequent
debutante parties, including the Cygnets' Ball,
the annual dance for a fashionable finishing school.

Try a London meal starting with smoked salmon or potted shrimp;
then have turbot or plaice or English sole with fresh vegetables, followed by
a savoury such as angels on horseback (oysters wrapped
in bacon on toast), or a Scotch woodcock (a dab of scrambled eggs
crisscrossed with anchovies). All this and more—plus fine Greek food—
is served at the White Tower (*right*) in Soho.

Not merely picturesque, the Cotswold countryside
in England reflects a beauty that is warm, kindly and profound.
Seen close up at Bourton-on-the-Water (*left*), the group-
ing of a house, a stream, a grove shows man and
nature in a deep, congenial harmony. At long range (*above*),
Barrington Village stretches placidly beside its rich meadowlands.

England's Cotswold life ignores the modern drive
toward change, finds its fulfillment in old and quiet
patterns. Instead of tabloid headlines, villagers
of Bibury (*above*) get all the news that's fit to
circulate by studying the public notice board. At
Little Rissington (*right*), a trainer breaks his hounds
in the gentle Cotswold way with a sixteen-mile
morning walk; he knows and calls each one by name
and the pups, less than a year old, already
run together like a veteran pack.

Polo is enjoying an exciting revival
in the British sporting scene, largely due
to the active participation and
genuine enthusiasm of the Duke of Edinburgh.

Blue sea, excellent sun, and a Riviera-like climate—
thanks to the gulf stream—attract thousands
of visitors to Torquay, a place of gardens, beaches
and gay terraces, and the largest of the
resort towns on England's South Devon coast.

Blazers, boaters, and flannels of oarsmen enliven the scene at England's renowned Henley rowing regatta held annually in early July.

The best of clothes, the best of people come to the Royal Meeting at Ascot for the annual races inaugurated by Queen Anne in 1711, where a bemedaled guard admits only the precious few to the Royal Enclosure.

Lord's, the hoary home of Britain's own game, cricket, achieves its sartorial and social pinnacle for a school event—the annual Eton-Harrow match.

Two young Britons in bright boaters attend their first Henley Royal Regatta. Henley's narrow course (*below*) finishes between the pavilions of the Leander and Phyllis clubs, at the end of the mile-and-570-yard "Henley distance." Princeton University's crew won the coveted Grand Challenge Cup in 1956.

Henley Royal Regatta, perhaps
the most cheerful sporting event in
England, is the greatest rowing event
in the world. A major social
occasion, too, it is a time
for reunion of old school friends,
wearing fine clothes, and Thames-side
family picnics. Cheering old
oarsmen in the stands,
darting shells on cool water,
fireworks and formal balls—
a sentimental bright spot
on London's sporting calendar.

Admission to the Royal Enclosure during the
Royal Meeting at Ascot is regarded
as a high social privilege and divorced persons
are still barred from the Queen's Lawn.

The parading of full fashion (*right and below*)
during the Ascot Meeting actually
outweighs the parading and racing of the
Thoroughbreds in popular interest.

40

IRELAND

IRELAND

The Rock of Cashel with its Round Tower, castle and other
antiquities, including the reputed coronation stone of ancient Munster
kings, is to be found at a confluence of roads in South Tipperary.

"The trouble with fellas that write about Ireland," said the sage of New York's Third Avenue, the man named Costello, "is that ye're loikely to be Dutch in the first place and prone to be leprechcorny. Further, the things you see there are loikely to be something else entirely. Iv'ry Irishman is his own grandfather, so that what you tell 'im is there today is completely in error compared to his own family memories and they accurate to the minute of the man recallin' thim. Now, bhoy, write sweetly of the One Land."

How else? For the names roll sweetly . . . Carlow, Cavan, Clare, Cork, Donegal, Galway, Kildare, Kilkenny, Limerick, Roscommon, Tipperary . . . all 32 of the counties, even the six in the North. Each spot of the Isle, with its greenest of green, the tang of peat fires, the hedgerows, the Gaelic signposts and the brash tales of Deirdre, Cuchulain and Maeve, is a home to those of the blood in no matter what land they exist. Thus, it follows that every part of Ireland, in terms of time, distance and filial remembrance, is a land of silver rivers where the salmon leap high, of kindly people, of a mystic past, of heroes all and the women beautiful. And fortunate is the tourist who accepts Ireland within the context of its own romance-colored eyes, for there is much to confirm that view. The pastoral life is the tempo of the country and the Glen of Two Lakes in County Wicklow is typical of that life. Nearby is the remainder of St. Kevin's monastery, a 6th Century edifice which speaks with the tongue of stone of early Christian missionaries, strangers to a land which blunted Roman swords but which once bent to an overflow of predatory Danes. More important to the site than the scattered remnants is the ancient cross of St. Kevin, for whosoever clasps his arms about it will have his every decent wish granted; proof enough that no matter what you see, it is likely to be something else entirely. But should the impossible happen, and the country life pall, there is always a metropolitan existence in Ireland, particularly in Dublin, where there is everything a visitor's heart could desire in pastimes and accommodations. Here, as always, the swans honk on the Liffey and Guinness refreshes while men talk of uprisings which are not of history but of vivid recollection, and of the great medical school of Dublin University whose library contains the fabulous Book of Kells, the 8th Century, illuminated manuscript which has been called the epitome of Irish art. This is an old land and a loved land and in any month Ireland is a place to be.

A barge floats into Limerick canal terminal.

Lough Allen in Leitrim County, near the
headwaters of the River Shannon, is the third largest—
eight miles long and three miles wide—of the
lakes formed by the river which is part of the southwestern
boundary of the county with Roscommon.
Grazing and agriculture are the principal occupations
of Leitrim—the field in the foreground boasts
a crop of that Irish staple, the potato.

For a city that has seen more turbulence than most any other in Europe, Dublin has an air of placid, solid charm. Above is O'Connell Street Bridge over the River Liffey.

A farmer accompanied by his dog drives his

Lord Mayor of Dublin, Denis Larkin, wears the traditional emblems of his office. He is the son of Jim Larkin, central character of Sean O'Casey's play, *Star Turns Red*.

cart through rolling countryside of County Cork.

Dublin is traditionally a city of legends and one is preserved by Susan Gaisford-St. Lawrence (*below*), whose family has held Howth Castle since 1174. A place at table is set to oblige a long-dead pirate queen. The beauty of Ireland's women, another Dublin tradition, is exemplified by Ann Gunning (*lower left*), of another famous family, modeling a Sybil Connelly dress.

Mrs. Brigid Enright, a characterful matron of some 74 years, lives with her daughter in an ancient thatched house near Ballylongford in County Kerry. Many such tidily thatched homes dot the Shannon countryside.

SCANDINAVIA

SCANDINAVIA

Hammerfest, in Norway, is the world's northernmost city but boasts
a mild climate due to the North Atlantic Drift. In spring great herds of reindeer
are swum across the Strömmen Strait to summer pasture in Seiland.

Bizarre sculpture of Gustav Vigeland
awes visitors to Frogner Park, in Oslo, Norway.

A young Lapp mother fondles her small son.

A chic Norwegian girl watches sailing race.

Sweden's Royal Palace, a baroque,
500-room, eighteenth-century, neoclassical
masterpiece, is a presence one seems never
able to avoid in all of Stockholm.
This view is from the Skeppsholmen bridge.

The most famous restaurant in Sweden, and
the largest in all Europe, is Berns,
in Stockholm. It is really three eating places
in one: French, Chinese, and Swedish.
At the right is the main dining room.

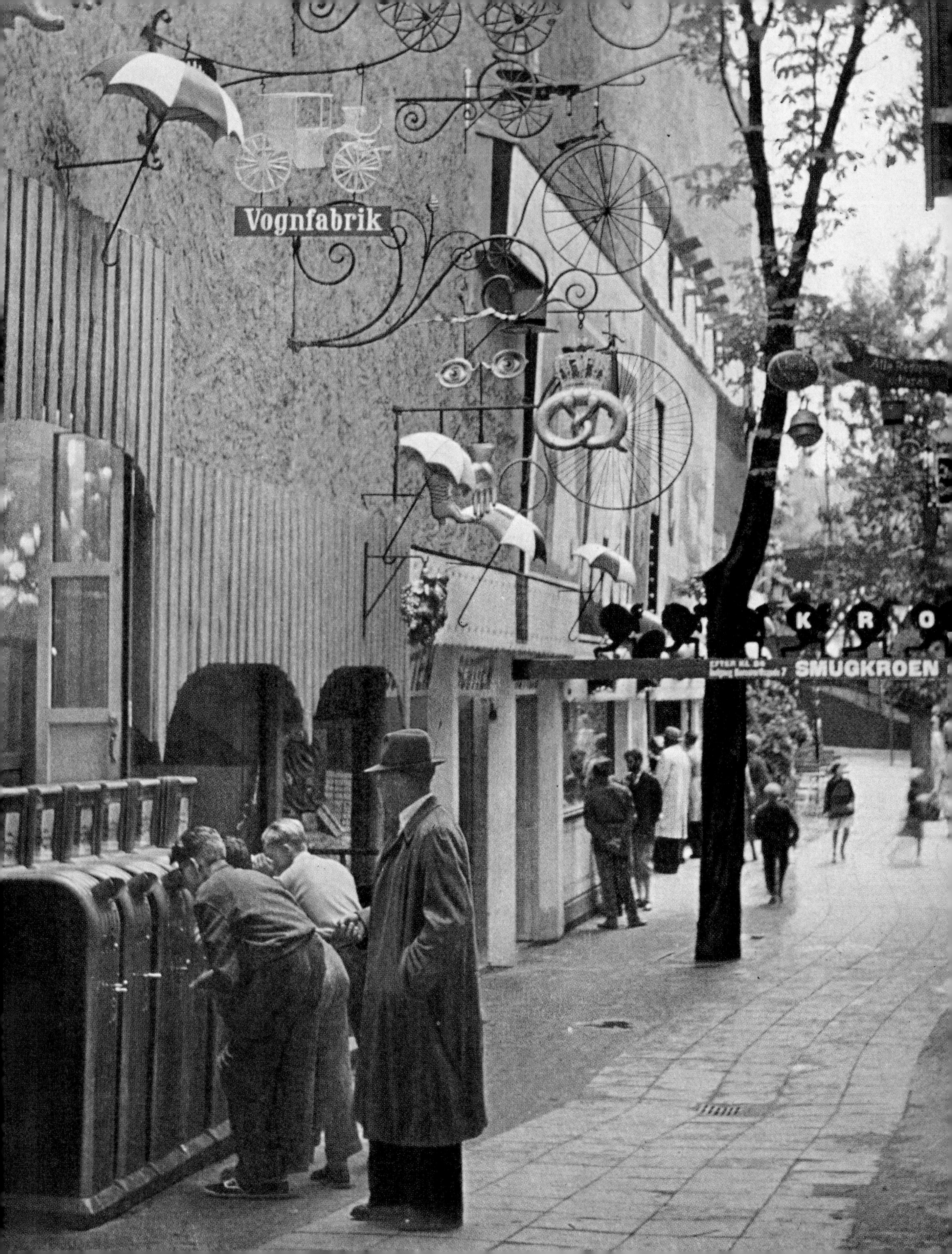
Vognfabrik
K R O
SMUGKROEN

Seafaring Denmark: Old women of
Fanø, one of the nation's many
ocean-minded islands, read their prayer
books under an exquisite ship's
model, one of five miniature vessels hanging
from the rafters of the old church.

Landlubber Denmark: Men sample the peep shows in
Tivoli Gardens, Copenhagen's beloved and beautiful pleasure park.
The signs outside the shops are traditional symbols of the
merchandise within, the pretzel (center) always designating a bakery.
Denmark also boasts the famous Royal Copenhagen porcelain factory
and the establishment of Georg Jensen, creator of hand-wrought silver.

The old roofs of Denmark's Ribe, once a seaport
and now an inland town, have changed little
since the Middle Ages; storks still nest here,
arriving on the same day every year.

An anchor at Nyhavn, Copenhagen's happy prowling grounds
for sailors, commemorates the seamen who died in
World War II. The oldest section in the city of Denmark,
Nyhavn is right on the edge of the canal.

Egeskov Mansion in Denmark rises from a lake on
Fünen, supported on deep-driven piles of oak.
The home of nobles since the 16th Century,
it sits on the gentle landscape like a
page from an Andersen fairy tale.

Small fry scamper past the home of
Hans Christian Andersen (*below*) on a quaint
street in Odense, on the island of Fünen.
He was not too fond of children, yet
his tales have delighted generations of them.

The Lapps of Norway
are nomadic,
drifting in small
groups from pasture
to pasture with
their reindeer.
They live in tents
and store
their possessions
in caches
suspended aloft.

THE LOW COUNTRIES

THE LOW
COUNTRIES

The windmills, forever a symbol of Holland,
turn merrily along the canals and, with dikes and electric pumps,
protect a land one fourth of which is below sea level.

One of our favorite characters is a tall, distinguished Dutchman. A businessman in temporary exile for profit, he spends much of his spare time correcting American opinion about The Netherlands. He is a perpetual-motion critic of author Mary Mapes Dodge and a gentle debunker of her book *Hans Brinker: or, The Silver Skates*. "This is a story," he says, "not a guidebook. No little Dutch boy ever plugged a leak in a dike with his finger. And don't tell me about the statue in Spaarndam to his memory. That's for politeness to tourists. Polite we always are. Quaint we ain't." There is little sense in explaining to him that Hans Brinker, like Hopalong Cassidy, is an American legend, or that May, for example, is a month in which every traveler has a right to wear the glaze of romance in his eyes. It's spring, even in 20th Century Holland, where hard-working electric pumps have largely replaced the windmill and bucket in the war against the sea. In the truthful, if romantic, tourist dream rosy-faced boys and girls in colorful costumes still eat cheeses, wear wooden shoes and gaze at fields ablaze with tulips. The diplomats and statesmen still confer with Queen Juliana in The Hague and the cyclists are wheeling north to the dunes and beaches of Scheveningen. Blue china is still being made along the cobbled streets of Delft, pottery first brought from China 300 years ago by the intrepid Dutch sailors and merchants who made the "hollow land" the pride of the civilized West during the 17th Century. Gouda (*see right*) is still a bustling market town, a household word with cheese lovers the world over. The Weepers' Tower still stands in Amsterdam where housewives once waved good-by to husbands off with Henry Hudson on the *Half Moon* to investigate New York and the Indians. This is the spotless land where even coal-mine structures are painted white. It is the land of Rembrandt, Jan Vermeer and Pieter de Hooch; and one of the easiest in all Europe to travel because it is so compact. The Netherlands, roughly half again as large as Massachusetts, can be traversed in a day, physically. The wise rover will choose to see Holland in terms of time, the remote village of Urk beached with the reclaimed lands of the Zuider Zee contrasted with the spanking postwar rejuvenation of Rotterdam . . . Giethoorn, where people move by canal and even cattle are ferried to pasture, contrasted with industrial Eindhoven . . . "God made the earth," says the old saw, "except Holland which the Dutchmen made for themselves," and a clean, comfortable, beautiful place it is to be.

You can think of Bruges in Belgium as a sort of northern, more Gothic Venice. It has its own canals—minus romantic gondoliers—and its very name is Flemish for bridges, which criss-cross canals and quays in architecturally charming profusion. Like its neighbor city Ypres, and like Venice, Bruges has a glorious commercial past dating back to the medieval days when commerce meant the mysterious East, ships loaded with treasure and tall tales from the remote Indies, piracy and pomp. Bruges had almost a monopoly of the important wool trade with England and was a staple center for the rich German Hanseatic League of merchant princes. Political, religious and economic changes, as well as the gradual silting over of its old harbor, sheared it of this prominence by the end of the 16th Century, but, like most cities that have known greatness, it has refused to turn its back on former glory. The monuments of Bruges' past are handsomely preserved and it has taken a new lease on life with a new harbor at Zeebrugge, increased trade and industry and a flourishing tourist traffic.

Bruges is the capital of West Flanders and has the easygoing and deceptively innocent charm of the blond *Flamande* about its personality. It faces across the Channel almost directly to the mouth of the Thames and its outward orientation had always been British. The nearby coast boasts a large English colony and the English may be held primarily responsible for its resort development. Generations of young and not-so-young ladies from the shires have sketched its cathedrals and bridges for the later edification of their friends at country house or parsonage. And with or without a sketchbook, the subjects are delightful to view. St. Sauveur and Notre Dame are both excellent examples of early Gothic at its best. The Groote Market is both bustling market place by day and the scene of band concerts on summer evenings. The Musée Communal is only one, but one of the best, repositories of early Flemish painting; it includes masterpieces by Jan van Eyck, Claeissens, Memling and other notables and cannot be missed by any serious student of the school.

The citizens of Bruges, naturally, are Flemish and your French will be adequate for communication, though you will find a large proportion of the people you meet, particularly in shops, restaurants and hotels, with a fluent command of English. Hotels there are aplenty, and pensions too. There are good restaurants in most of the hotels as well as some outstanding independent cafés. The two best ways to see Bruges most rewardingly are on foot and by boat, and you will want to do both. As in any new city, you will want to hunt out some of its hidden byways on your own. For the rest, rent yourself one of the pleasure boats which ply the canals— your hotel can make arrangements—and see the city as it should be seen in the whole, from its waterways.

Bruges is perfect in June, when its summer is just beginning, when the flowers in its bright-hued markets are at their loveliest, when it offers the fullest reward to the visitor from far away.

With a landscape redolent of a Grimm's fairy tale, the Grand Duchy of Luxembourg has found it impossible to avoid a certain pixie flavor. Actually, it hasn't tried. It dotes on picturesque ruins, the Little People, ghostly accursed horsemen. In its 999 square miles (thirty-seven miles at the widest, sixty-two at the longest), smaller than Rhode Island, Luxembourg religiously preserves 130 ruined castles. All possess the same piquant aura of medieval gloom and romance that characterizes 13th Century Vianden at your right; all are haunted. In Luxembourg, the autumn season of the boar hunt is just the time to gather round the hearth after the kill and trade ghastly fairy stories. With all 300,000 Luxembourgers in the grip of such pleasant morbidity, the entire country is what the French would call *un type*, or, as we would say, a character.

But Luxembourgers don't give a hoot what the French or anyone else calls them, so long as they aren't called Frenchmen, Germans or Belgians. Sandwiched between France, Germany and Belgium, and grabbed or about-to-be-grabbed by all of them at one time or another, Luxembourg remains fiercely itself, as its two-division army of 2400 men stands ready to prove at the drop of a casque. The rugged individualism of its founding father Sigefroid, who married a river sprite and sold his soul to the devil, has come down untarnished since A.D. 963. The favorite line of Luxembourg's favorite song runs, "*Mir woelle bleiwe wat mir sin*," meaning, bluntly, "We want to remain what we are."

Neighbors who have looked on Luxembourg as a fairyfied little pushover have learned differently. When the country was once incorporated into the Lowlands, its delegates stubbornly refused to raise more than one finger, instead of the accustomed two, in taking the oath of fealty. And when the Nazis invaded Luxembourg in World War II and attempted to make the entire populace sign a declaration stating they were Germans and their mother tongue German, the answer was a ringing universal no. They were Luxembourgers and their mother tongue *letzeburgesch*. Though this language sounds like German enunciated through a mouthful of smoked pork and lentils, Luxembourg's national dish, it is incomprehensible to Germans and is an *independent* language, not a dialect. When the Nazis further attempted to conscript the Luxembourg youth, they were met with nationwide defiance and the first underground resistance of Occupied Europe.

Luxembourgers may love their fairy stories, but they also know how to squeeze that old happy ending out of the bitterest reality.

Dressed in her unchanging native costume—lace cap, heavy frilled dress, red coral necklace—pretty, 12-year-old Wolmoed ("Woltje") Jonk looks like a storybook Dutch girl as she blows a dandelion plucked from the banks of the dike bordering the Zuider Zee at the town of Volendam.

CENTRAL EUROPE

CENTRAL EUROPE

Mont-Saint-Michel, the great "citadel in the sea," is connected with
the mainland of France by a mile-long causeway. The magnificent Gothic abbey,
founded in 708, is visited by thousands of travelers each year.

No city's name breathes quite so much magic as Paris. Although she has celebrated her two-thousandth birthday, to her devotees—and they number many millions—she remains ever young, charming and unpredictable.

It is probably absurd to think of Paris in terms of a particular time of year. Any such selection, the popularity of *April in Paris*, *Paris in the Spring*, *et al.* to the contrary notwithstanding, will bring anguished cries from Parisians and Parisians by adoption that their city is an eighth world wonder the year round. We choose July only as a matter of convenience, convenience to the traveler whose summer vacation plans suit this month best, to the traditionalist who feels Bastille Day (July 14) should be celebrated on the spot, to everyone who loves the vast and various city in warm weather, with open windows, sidewalk cafés in full bloom, the Queen of Cities in the casual climate of romance and relaxation.

Paris has become a special symbol of intelligence, art and sophistication. Despite wars, depressions, political crises, and frenzied fluctuation of the franc, it has held, sometimes with a certain feminine truculence, to its position as world capital of culture. To Paris went the young American painters and writers of the early 1920's; most of them to enrich their own heritage, to return to America stronger in their art, better able to interpret the meaning of their homeland. Gertrude Stein spoke for them when she said, "America is my country, but Paris is my home town." There had been Americans in love with Paris long before, there are young and eager American artists in Paris today. There are also Englishmen, White Russians, Tonkinese, Mexicans, Sikhs, Germans, Siamese, Moors, Finns, Basques, everyone of every race.

Paris is a city for everyone, from the student-adventurer on his own to the tight-knit family seeking to expose Junior and Sissie to the best of the Old World. There is history on every street, from the pomp and splendor of the Tuileries to the *faubourgs* that still recall the barricades of 1848, from memories of the glittering corruption of the Stavisky scandal to memories of Roman legions garrisoning an island city in barbarian Gaul, from the swashbuckling romance of Dumas' musketeers to the precise and monumental engineering of the Eiffel Tower.

There is Art, of course, from the time-tried masterpieces of the Louvre to the studios and galleries of the moderns. There is fine eating, the cuisine that has become world-synonymous with gastronomical excellence. There is high fashion, still the highest and most influential in the world.

Paris lives, strongly, gaily, brightly. After 2000 years of playing hostess to the world, she is still hospitable and gracious, able to please, charm, instruct and gratify the millions magnetized by the magic of her name and fame.

It's every woman's dream to buy a creation direct from a famous couturier. A Dior mannequin models a rose tulle dress with professional nonchalance. Place du Tertre (*left*), once the public square of the village of Montmartre, is now packed with a heavy concentration of artists and restaurants. Parked by the curb is a hot-rod, Paris version, while in the background rise the spires of the Sacré-Coeur.

Grand Elegance, Parisian style, is rarer these days, but there is still a handful of great balls and festive occasions where Paris society can rise to its old, eye-filling glory. The tail-coated princes and handsomely gowned *comtesses* on this page were photographed at a *grand bal* given by Bolivian tin heir Antenor Patino, at his beautifully furnished Paris home. Four hundred guests waltzed in a specially built outdoor ballroom covered with a canopy of rose silk, chatted under illuminated trees, ate from 18th Century silver service, and remembered *le temps d'autrefois*. In the forest at Chantilly (*opposite page*), in a setting reminiscent of a Degas painting, top-hatted Thoroughbred owners talk with their jockeys before a big stakes race at the Chantilly race course. For the same socialites, the gardens of the Ritz (*bottom, opposite*) are an attractive and popular rendezvous for luncheon in the springtime.

Moulin Rouge, old stand-by cabaret near Place Pigalle,
now offers a rather sedate variety show.

Women and mechanical marvels get equal billing at the famed
Folies-Bergère and are combined here nicely in the *Bird in a Gilded Cage*
number. Probably the best-known music hall in the world, and
famous for the elaborateness of its shows, with some
three hours of beauty, music and color, the Folies Bergère
is high on the list of Paris tourist attractions.

To re-create the elegance of Versailles for the picture
at right, one of the stately rooms of the Grand Trianon
was especially furnished with authentic pieces.
Chairs and sofa are signed by the 18th Century cabinetmaker,
Jean Baptiste Lebas, and covered in a modern copy of
a treasured 1760 brocade that is seldom exhibited.
The vista from the Allée de l'Été (*below*) in the gardens of
Versailles emphasizes the sweeping scope and attention
to detail that sets them apart from all others.

The river Loire meanders through central France like a casual but knowing traveler who has learned how to get the most out of highway and byway, city and plain. Unfolding on either side of it is some of France's and the world's most beautiful and rewarding countryside, rich in pleasure for the tourist, in historic tradition and in culinary delights for the gourmet.

The Loire is no mean river; it runs through seven provinces and stretches some 645 miles from source to mouth. From below Le Puy in Haute Loire it flows northwest, turning more sharply toward the west at Orleans and flowing onward to the sea through Blois and Tours and Angers and Nantes to empty into the Bay of Biscay at St.-Nazaire. The names themselves are an itinerary trumpeting history, pleasure and romance. Look at your map near where the river makes its great curve and you'll find Meung, a name like the clash of a musketeer's sword against a villain's helm plate, the town where D'Artagnan first encountered Milady DeWinter.

The whole valley is crowded with sights and entertainments for the traveler. Near the first waters of the river lie some of the finest châteaux in France, a glimpse of the aristocratic splendor of the days of the Sun King and before. The Renaissance château (*on opposite page*) lies in the valley plain traced by the river Cher at Villandry. It was built about 1532 by Jean LeBreton, a courtier of François I and has been superbly restored both without in its formal landscaping and inside with treasures of 16th Century art. Other châteaux, not only of courtiers but of the royal family of France itself, spread through the valley as it climbs northward. Orleans and Bourges boast monumental cathedrals. Elsewhere along the way are dungeons and ancient redoubts for connoisseurs of the ancient and romantic past.

A special chapter could be written, indeed has, by literary gastronomes, on the wines and the cuisine of the Loire Valley. Grapes grow along the riversides and their pressings yield such treasures as Coulée de Serrant, Coteaux du Layon, adaptable Vouvray and other liquid delights. Also for the table, the region is famous for its lark pies, its crow soup, the fine white butter of Anjou, which is a savory sauce of melted butter, vinegar, shallots, salt and pepper. Pork and goose dishes achieve immortality here, and the hunters' haven of Sologne offers game delicacies cooked in a thousand different ways to delight the palate. Even to list the specialties of different localities—sausages from Gâtinais, poached eggs in Vouvray jelly from the Touraine, stuffed fish of Anjou, to name only a few—would take a considerable amount of space.

There isn't much doubt about it, the Loire Valley is a cornucopia of variety and delight, with hospitable accommodations for travelers, diversion ranging from sport to scholarship, a sunny and mild climate, and beauty on every side.

Faith that abides: St. Martin's window
in the famed Chartres Cathedral
glows (*at left*), the gift of 13th Century
shoemakers; (*above*), Cathedral and
town; (*right*), the Nativity story in gemlike
panels of 12th Century work.

The Annunciation

The Visitation

The Nativity

The Angels and the Shepherds

The Magi

Welcoming the Magi

Presentation at the Temple

Herod ordering the Slaughter

The Flight into Egypt

Château Chambord,
near Blois,
is one of France's
famous castles.
Favorite residence
of Francis I,
it is noted for its
winding staircase
and remarkable
Renaissance
architecture. The
castle of Richard
the Lion-Hearted,
(*right*), in Normandy,
is a startling
reminder of the
Middle Ages
and has walls
ranging from eight
to fifteen feet
in thickness.

Off Marseilles lies the island bastion Château d'If (*above*), made famous by Dumas' *Count of Monte Cristo*. The fort, built in 1529, contrasts sharply with the new Le Corbusier apartments (*right*) which the Marseillais first looked at in awe. The water front (*far right*) is in the resort town of Cassis, a few miles below Marseilles.

Switzerland knows winter down to the latest overlap of freshly pure snow, down to the last crisp breeze stinging your cheek before you dodge into the friendly shelter of an Alpine lodge, down to the white stillness of a mountain night broken only by the crackle of frozen crust beneath a passer-by's foot. As a tourist haven, of course, Switzerland offers charm the whole year round. Its clean, high hamlets have long been a lure both to health seekers and to casual holidayers from all over the world. Golf, tennis, shooting and fishing, in summer, spring and fall, attract their addicts. Its busy cities and its stouthearted citizenry have held the little nation fast as an important and anything but isolated island of neutrality through mankind's most terrible wars. From cuckoo clocks to fine timepieces to masterpieces of precision engineering, its craftsmanship has been renowned for generations. To a country generously endowed by nature with some of the most magnificent scenery to be found anywhere in the world, the Swiss have brought an indestructible passion for hard work. Switzerland is the result.

There are probably more comfortable times to see Switzerland than in midwinter and yet we vote for the land when the snow lies upon it. For winter is the season when the mountains which are Switzerland's pride, her most ancient defense and her timeless adornment, come fully into their own. Then tiny towns like Grindelwald (*opposite*) in twisting mountain valleys take on a special beauty. Snow curves and shields them warmly, thatching the picture-book houses with a man-high extra layer of glistening white. Here, in the Swiss heartland, the old customs which have never died, songs and festivals and dances in native dress unchanged for ages, seem fitting and true and integral to life and the scene around them. These are villages with room for elves as well as for humans, hills where all the sleet-bright mythology of winter becomes believable, from St. Nicholas to the erlking.

There are simpler and less faerie lures for the winter traveler in Switzerland, for the Alpine nation can make a firm claim to being the original winter-sports capital of the world. The mountain slopes are webbed with ski tows and all the classic runs are brave with would-be ski-meisters. From December through February, and sometimes from late October to early May and later at the higher resorts, fine skiing is in season, with experts from the farthest climes competing. So, too, with skating, both on artificial rinks and on outdoor ponds and lakes, and with free-style tobogganing and bobsledding. The languages of some forty or fifty nations speak the tribal tongue of the sport. Here a Georgian prince compares a snow tan with a duchess still dark from the Riviera while an enthusiast from New Hampshire gossips with an English expert about the technique of a visiting maharaja.

At catering to the wants and pleasures of the tourist, the Swiss are past masters; their reputation as hosts and innkeepers goes back as far as the history of travel for pleasure. Not only in the larger cities but even in the less frequented towns you will find clean and comfortable lodging; and Swiss food, partaking of the excellences of French, Italian and German cuisines, has long made gourmets' mouths water. It is no coincidence that you will find Swiss or Swiss-trained hotel managers in spots as little Alpine as the Persian Gulf or the luxury coast of Florida. Switzerland has been a training ground for superior innkeepers for years, and all that this bespeaks in convenience is there for the visiting traveler.

So whether it's for the wonders of winter scenery, for elfin nostalgia, for robust snow sports or for the sheer creature comforts of a nation which has learned how to cater to tourists, we give you Switzerland.

St. Moritz, Europe's smartest winter resort,
lies snug in the Engadine Valley of the Swiss Alps.
Noon finds the Hotel Steffani restaurant astir
with snow and ice fans, lunching, laughing,
and listening to accordion-accompanied yodelers.

Figure skaters practice on the ice rink at the Kulm hotel to the strains of gay music. Large Swiss hotels have their own ice rinks for skating enthusiasts.

Spectators watch an international ski race at St. Moritz surrounded by mountains of breath-taking beauty. The site of several Olympic winter games, this magnificent Swiss resort achieved fame only after two Norse students "discovered" it in 1885.

The icy peak of the Matterhorn
in the Swiss Alps, 14,780 feet high,
has been scaled by more than 50,000 men,
women and children—and one cat! At its base
lies the lovely resort village of Zermatt.

Zurich, Switzerland's largest city, looking downstream along the Limmat River. Both banks are lined with fine

old façades, including two 13th Century churches (*left*) and the venerable Gross-Münster or Cathedral (*right*).

Clinging to peaks just above the Lake of Lucerne is the
breath-taking Swiss resort, the Bürgenstock Estate.
The roomy Palace and Park hotels and swimming pool (*left*)
shine in the bright Swiss sunlight. Nearby (*above*) is the resort's
scary and popular Hammetschwand Lift, an elevator
that speeds guests up to the top of Bürgenstock Mountain.

Switzerland's clean, high hamlets
have long been a lure
both to health seekers and
to casual holidayers
from all over the world.
Here, dominating the picturesque
little harbor on Lake Thun,
is Spiez, with its ancient
castle—a medieval structure
with an 11th Century basilica.

The mountains of Switzerland are the country's special beauty, as well as the defender of the world's most unique peace. From Kleine Scheidegg (*below*) a railway climbs through tunnels to the 11,333-foot saddle (*upper center*) of the Jungfrau.

When weather becomes oppressive in Europe, knowing travelers take to the hills. Specifically, the Alps and especially those rugged, snow-capped, forest-draped peaks which spill over from Austria and Switzerland into southern Germany or Bavaria.

Here the *Ausländer* comes, heat jaded from the gayer boulevards, perhaps, or soul weary from cities, to take the waters at Bad Tolz or Bad Heilbrun. He comes to swim in Lake Wesslinger, sail on the Chiem-See, to climb the soaring Sonnstagshorn or to marvel at the crystal splendor of the Königs-See. He comes, perhaps, merely to visit with the *Alpensleber* busy tending their upland herds or carving exquisite figurines out of wood or making some of the world's finest violins at Mittenwald. For this is romance country in the great traditions of tourist Europe. Its historic peace is manifest in the village of Oberammergau where every decade for three centuries the pageant of the Passion Play has expressed the gratitude of a people spared the 17th Century ravages of the Black Death.

Not all of the pageantry of Bavaria is religious, of course. As the *Grossmutter* of a HOLIDAY editor once said, "Bavaria is some gayer too." The country is full of its "some gayer" past. Its costumes are colorful with the traditional Alpine *Lederhosen* and dirndl much in evidence at pastoral festivities. Its beer is golden, hearty and topped with a suds robust enough to support the flowing mustaches of some of its drinkers. Its dances are active as befits a folk with mountain-climbing muscles. Its peaks are dappled with castles, towered, walled and as massive as Neuschwanstein (pictured at the right) which was built by the utterly regal, if blandly daffy, King Ludwig II, a decade before he was led off to an asylum. Ludwig II at least left a monument of beauty, which is more than Bavaria got from a more vicious maniac, Hitler, who chose a peak at Berchtesgaden on which to build an eyrie.

But drama takes many forms in the uplands. It is as diverse as the music of Richard Wagner, who finished *Der Ring des Nibelungen* under the spell of the granite peaks. It may be as thrilling as a ski run when winter turns the Bavarian Alps into a sportsmen's paradise and resort areas like Garmisch-Partenkirchen, site of the 1936 winter Olympics, bustle with skiers from all over Europe, most of them festive on a sun-tan and oxygen binge in the shadow of the Zugspitze—Germany's highest (9722 feet). "Festive" is the word for Bavaria, and summer or winter, in this land of *Gemütlichkeit* and the yodel, the traveler is king and the *Inländer* a traditional and effortless host. Up steins and *prosit!*

From the Vosges Mountains of France to its confluence with the Rhine at Coblenz, Germany, the Moselle River cuts a 320-mile valley through the heartland and history of Europe. Thus creating, as a very wise and naughty old gentleman once told us, the only region in the world that has managed to put 2000 years of civilization into long, slim, green bottles. "Mankind," he pontificated, "can only be endured when it is seen through something as utterly gay, light and dry as Moselle wines. The grape is eternal." There is much to be said for such a viewpoint on the Moselle Valley. The Romans were planting vines along the shallow, twisting river two millenniums ago and there is scarcely a single one of the toy villages and towns (*see right*) strung along the Moselle's banks that does not have its terraces lifted to the sun today, vineyards glowing with color, grape leaves shining blue-green by the chemical consent of insect spray, set against the brighter green-brown lacework of the vines. So venerated is the vineyard in both its allegorical sense and as a form of sustenance to the hard-working dwellers of the long valley that tourists today may see in a quiet vineyard chapel at Ediger a medieval carving of Christ crushed beneath a symbolic wine press, His blood mingled with the wine.

Such sunshine devotions are not confined to the fields and terraces along the Moselle. This is also a valley of churches, of ancient monasteries and shrines. Trier, Germany's oldest city and once the capital of the Roman Empire, holds the Basilica of St. Matthew, the only grave of an apostle north of the Alps. It would be a foolhardy traveler who attempted to pick any "best" within the valley scope, either in vintage, sights or points of interest. A HOLIDAY correspondent once queried a canoeist about his impressions of the river and was told, "Herr American, I am not even sure that now is today on the Mosel."

The ancient in terms of old Roman gates, tombs, fortifications and the medieval expressed in hilltop castles, bridges and unchanged towns do give the immediate present an ephemeral tinge. It is not wine alone that would lead the visitor to expect the momentary appearance of a Roman poet, an archbishop, a prince elector. The atmosphere of the valley is heady with more than grape. So much so that one of our photographers once told us that when he reached the Rhine at Coblenz and saw a diesel barge grunting a mundane commercial haul past the fortress of Ehrenbreitstein he felt like weeping at the reminder of the outside world. He would have, too, except that he kept remembering a hillside at Cochem, the clink of glasses and a chorus of vineyard workers singing to the accompaniment of an accordion.

When the Kaiser Wilhelm Memorial Church
is restored, one tower will remain a ruin.

Roco Hacienda, formerly a Spanish film set,
is now an outdoor Berlin café by the water.

Glass cases display merchandise enticingly
and add to the luster of Hardenbergstrasse.

Coal barges, approaching the Berlin Cathedral
on the River Spree, add Old World color.

Two teams of horses, one real, the other splashed on a wall in Salzburg, add to the delightfully festive air that, surprisingly, extends even to commerce in Austria.

Heiligenblut is pilgrimage town in Carinthia near the cloud-flanked Grossglockner, Austria's highest peak.

Lovely Traun Lake, near Salzburg, is favorite resort of exiled kings as well as of rumpled visitors from local farms.

Austria's famous White Horse Inn at St. Wolfgang is a gay place with its own landing stage on the Wolfgangsee.

A Tirolean bull wears festive headgear on the way home from summer pasture in the highlands to winter quarters.

Innsbruck: A banner-draped street faces the "gold roof" balcony, with the vast Nordkette towering beyond.

The girls of Dürnstein wear traditional golden caps. This Danube village is wonderful wine-growing area.

A hunter and his family cross a mountain meadow in the scenic Salzkammergut lake country in central Austria.

Tirolean women lend the ox a willing hand at harvest time in the meadows—73% of the country is mountainous.

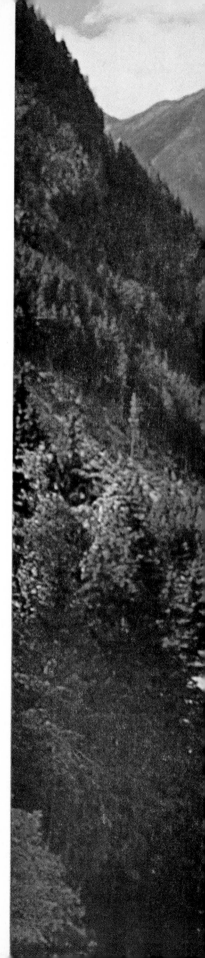

Austria's Tyrol is a salient of towering Alps and green valleys which juts majestically into Western Europe along the adjoining borders of Germany to the north and Italy to the south. Its westernmost province, Vorarlberg, touches Switzerland, producing mixed emotions among the thrifty Swiss, who would just as soon see this year's bumper crop of tourists stay within Switzerland's borders instead of romping off into the musical-comedy reaches of the Tyrol.

The Tyrol, however, has been a tourist land since Rome's legions walked through the Brenner Pass long before the Messrs. Hitler and Mussolini plotted disaster within its craggy walls. Its Alp-wrinkled reaches of stark peaks and post-card valleys are inhabited by a sturdy, fun-loving people divided equally into persons with imperial Hapsburg noses and cousins of HOLIDAY's Ludwig Bemelmans. Author Bemelmans, a literary refugee from the business of alpine innkeeping, is remembered fondly in some sections of the freedom-sacred Tyrol as a twinkling rump vanishing over an Alp pursued by the Gestapo.

The Tyrol is a land of goat and cattle herders during the cool mountain summers and ski instructors during the white and much cooler winters. It is famed for mountain climbers, yodelers and the obscure designer who gave the world the Tyrolean hat. It is also the land of the embroidered suspender, the ornate belt and the *Lederhosen*, the leather shorts which, accompanied by wool knee socks and smock coats, have adorned the casts of *The Student Prince* and sundry costume gauds since the discovery of the chorus boy. Further, the Tyrol is the native home of the dirndl, the flowered shawl and the braided halo hairdo, appurtenances which transform all *Mädel* into Teutonic visions of loveliness. It is the country of Enzian schnapps, a liquor made from the wild blue gentian which taken in regular doses can make the *Gross Glockner*, Austria's highest peak (12,461 feet), look like a half hour's climb.

Tourist Tyrol, the beer-drinking land of the dancing, thigh-slapping *Schuhplattler*, where the archduke always marries the pure but beautiful goatherd girl, is, in a sense, a wonderful myth. For the most part the thousands of visitors find the trappings of the myth valid. Meadows ablaze with flowers contrast with dark green forests. Ancient villages show their fairy-tale buildings against the battlements of the Alps. The ice-cold streams, born in glaciers, water the valleys where women stand waist-high in growing hay.

The Tyrolese are good hosts with a festive tradition, and the physical terrain is forever a matchless yeartime idyll. The wintertime skier, brushing up the Arlberg technique, which expatriate Hannes Schneider brought to the United States through Dartmouth College, will delight in the pristine slopes and snug inns.

In a trilingual land of rare beauty, the spirit of the Austrian Tyrol is still best expressed in the gentle hailing "*Grüss Gott*"—greet God. After all, He is always in the heights.

The small Austrian village of Lech am Arlberg, one of many in a radius of fifty miles, frost-decorated by the deep, powdery, and constant snow. Its mountain slopes are webbed with ski tows and all the classic runs are brave with would-be ski-meisters.

THE IBERIAN PENINSULA

THE IBERIAN PENINSULA

The walled city of Obidos, founded by the Celts some 300 years
before Christ, surveys the fields about it and contributes
to the richness and variety of Portugal's countryside.

Portugal, on the map, looks a little like New Jersey plastered against the western coastline of Spain. This impression is entirely deceptive, for the visitor will find Portugal a proudly independent nation, once ruler of half the New World and still conscious of this heritage, a handsome, quirky country aggressively willing to invite comparison of its special treasures of art, literature and living with those of any other land.

Portugal offers rich variety, both in its cities and its countryside. Lisbon has been, since before World War I, one of the international capitals of the world. Its prominence in Western eyes was pointed up most sharply during the last war when Portuguese neutrality made it a glamorous center of spies, diplomats, refugees, newspapermen and world figures from all the warring nations. But long before this, when Vasco da Gama set sail from its harbor to explore, discover and claim distant lands across the seas for Portugal, Lisbon had renown. Its pastel buildings—pink and blue and green and white—hang from its hillsides with precarious charm. Its hotels, as befit an international focal point, are among the world's most luxurious. Its restaurants and cafés run the gamut of national tastes, from the almost Kasbah retreats of the Moorish quarter, where native singers chant their indigo *fados* of love and death, to smart American bars where your very dry Martini will be blessed with just a twist of lemon.

Portugal's playland is along its coast, its own Portuguese Riviera. West of Lisbon are Estoril, Csacais and Sintra, comfortable in climate, green and luxurious, supplied with continental tourist lures from magnificent beachland to golf courses and a casino. Heading south, one finds still more beaches, 50 handsome miles of them from Sagres to Faro, as yet less developed than those in the Estoril region, but more splendid in their natural beauty than anything man could hope to improvise. Pensions and hotels are less plentiful in this area but the spacious, crowd-free beaches, the off-trail fishing villages, the exotic regional cookery, more than balance this for the discriminating visitor. This whole southern province, the Algarve, directly opposite Morocco, is African in feeling and influence, a joy to behold when its famed almond trees are in full blossom.

A major virtue of Portugal for the tourist is its size. It is large enough to contain the almost endless variety hinted at above, and yet, since it measures only 350 by 140 miles at its widest, you can cover all its points of interest and amusement in a conveniently short time. From the metropolitan business of Lisbon or the resort luxury of Estoril, you can skip quickly and easily to the rural vistas of Estremadura, for example.

Portugal's main cities offer modern accommodations and its equable climate seldom goes to extremes—around 55° in winter and 70° in summer. Only 15 hours from New York, it is a happy compromise between tropic heat and mountain snows, a haven for the traveler who refuses to haunt only beaten pathways.

Peasant women gather at Viana do Castelo, in the far north of Portugal, to watch the dancing during one of the city's pulsing, colorful fairs. Women wear their most vivid best for the occasion.

Fishermen of Nazaré, up the coast from Lisbon, mend their nets on the beach as the gentle Atlantic fog rolls in. The Portuguese character is one of reserve and dignity, even in dress, yet men of this region fancy the eye-catching local checks.

The Portuguese country-
side is stony but gentle,
a tawny terrain
where peasants go
about their labors
peacefully with donkeys
and windmills
to aid them.
This frugal village
lies on the back road
that connects
cosmopolitan Estoril
and Cintra.

Fifty miles northwest of blue-white Cádiz on the Atlantic coast, and seventy-odd south of Seville, lies the quiet, ancient city of Arcos de la Frontera. And, in terms applicable to any other place, particularly any in the United States, nothing is going on there—nothing, that is, but the clearly discernible passage of time, and the routine events attendant upon a Spanish appreciation of mortality. But *poco á poco*, knowing stateside travelers are remembering Andalusia and Arcos (*see left*), perhaps encouraged by the raw rains of a March at home and long, long thoughts of the Bureau of Internal Revenue. Like many of the old *frontera* communities—so called because they were on the borderline of Moorish-Spanish territory—most of the town sprawls on the slope of a huge sandstone bluff. It is an implausibly henna-hued bluff in the bold sunshine, which glints off the water of the river Gaudelete. From the church tower at its highest point, the city winds down to the valley floor step by step, the flat roofs which serve as back yards and the enclosed patios of old Moorish design glowing bright red and stark white in the crystal air and limitless light. In Arcos, as in many another town once occupied by the Moors, the people who "built like giants and finished like jewelers" made streets narrow; buildings could thus provide a measure of shade. Gay blades of Andalusia long ago learned to appreciate the city planning of the ancient enemy for lighter reasons. A *Holiday* correspondent once ran all over Andalusia, half oblivious to olive groves, blossoming orange trees and old Roman architecture, looking for streets called *callejón del beso*—"kiss lanes" so narrow that lovers standing on opposite balconies can take advantage of a situation. But there is a much graver emotion in the serene towns of Andalusia at certain times of year. Lent, for example, comes to an end in the great and solemn pageantry of Holy Week. In Arcos there will be the immemorial procession, and soaring voices will rise from the choir gallery of Santa Maria de la Asunción. Compared to the glories of the Faith as expressed elsewhere to the Passion of the Lord—in Seville, in Cádiz, in Granada, Cartagena and Málaga—the reverence of Arcos, while equally deep, is not quite as demonstrative. But all of Spain is on its knees during Holy Week, and wherever there are men, in villages, towns and cities, art and beauty and emotion pay tribute commemorating the drama of Golgotha. Spain again remembers that there is more to life than brave Miura bulls in Andalusia, more than figs and cork oak, more than the nutlike wines of Jerez, more than fiesta and siesta. And while Spain remembers, it is likely that the visitor from the west, eye-rich with the lush and varied delights of an old and often delightful land, will find time to reappraise his own being.

The past is always close at hand in Spain, ready to take over the new and merge it into history. Even the newly erected arrows of the Spanish Falange (*above*) fade quickly into an old wall, where an old peasant rests. Outside Ávila (*right*), the present-day landscape of a stone-colored, stone-walled city, simple stone cross and shepherds riding asses might be a Spanish scene painted hundreds of years ago by Goya, Velásquez or El Greco.

Arrogance and elegance, love of ritual and love of spectacle,
preoccupation with death and emotion and courage—
all these make up the most Spanish of all Spanish pastimes, the bullfight—
are visible in the faces of the Madrid *toreros at the left*.
Above, the jam-packed stands of the Seville ring.

The Spain of romance, of guitars and castanets, of mantillas,
roses and dark-eyed girls, is still visible to the tourist
who looks for it. In Seville (*below*), girls of the old quarter
dress in ancient flamenco costume in preparation
for the April Feria. In Cordoba (*right*), an old grilled courtyard
sparkles with color as the bright Spanish sunlight falls
on roses and geraniums and a warmly tiled floor.

A castle in Spain
and a great one—
the mighty
Alcazar of Segovia.
Built in the
14th century, it
was a bright
center of Spain's
world empire.

There is nothing gentle or easy about the countryside of Spain, which perhaps explains why it has changed so little since the days of those celebrated Spanish travelers, Don Quixote and Sancho Panza (*above*, in a Madrid statue). In Granada (*right*), the little houses of a small, stony town huddle closely together against the arid vastness of its surrounding mountains.

Palma, Mallorca's biggest city, skirts the shore of its beautiful bay. Surrounded by picturesque hills and blessed with a pleasant year-round climate, it has become one of Europe's most popular resorts.

THE MEDITERRANEAN

THE MEDITERRANEAN

Monte Carlo is one of three villages in the tiny Principality of Monaco. Built on a rocky promontory jutting into the Mediterranean, it has long been known in song and story for its legendary gaming casinos and, more recently, for the marriage of its Prince Rainier to Miss Grace Kelly of Philadelphia.

Varied are the lures of travel. A second-generation Italian-American, a Fifth Army veteran once quartered in an officers' rest camp at Stresa on the shores of Italy's Lake Maggiore, was heard to remark, "All my life I heard about Maggiore, Lugano, Como and di Garda," he said. "To this day when I listen to my father the Lombard Lakes are heaven with money, all blue and gold with tropical flowers and magnificent people. When I was there during the war. . . . Well, can you imagine Miami Beach during the Renaissance? So I have to go back to find out for sure." Such Latin sentiment has been valid since the Romans knew this forty-mile reach of water which stretches from the southern ramparts of the Swiss Alps to a point only thirty miles north of Milan, jump-off city for most tourists headed into the lake region of Northern Italy. Some member of the hardy international set is always going back to Lake Maggiore to confirm a memory or build a new one. It could be an Ernest Hemingway, a Princess Margaret Rose, a gaggle of diplomats remembering Locarno and a distant peace or an Arturo Toscanini staving off the outside world from his rented island of San Giovanni. Pinpointing beauty along the shores of Maggiore (*see opposite page*) is a bootless task for a collector of superlatives, but no visitor will leave the area without some opulent impression of the Borromean Islands, named for the Italian nobility who transformed them from rocky islets to subtropical gardens. The loveliest of them all (a perennial café argument) is Isola Bella. It was Count Vitaliano Borromeo who planted the earth with exotic shrubs, subtropical trees and all the flowers the world of his time could supply. The whole island became a garden of ten terraces, the lowest built on piles driven into the lake, and filled with statuary and fountains, many originals which remain today along with the baroque Palazzo Borromeo where Vitaliano once played host to royalty. Today's visitors can still see the Murano glass, the Flemish tapestries, the Viennese porcelains and the latter-day tracks of time which include the bed that Napoleon usurped during his Italian campaign and the conference room (once the music hall) used by Mussolini in the 30's. But palaces and gardens and villas and cafés, indigenous as they are to Maggiore, have a ghostly quality in the Italian summer moonlight. Then, as it may have been in the beginning, there are only the limned peaks against the milky sky and the shining blue waters and a nightbird singing in an orange tree.

A church procession, ending the Madonna del Carmine festival, weaves
through the narrow streets of Rome's Trastevere quarter, whose
people claim to be the oldest, truest Romans. Handsome *carabinieri* (*left*)
patrol the streets of Rome in pairs. Here one gallantly assists
two American Embassy girls on their sight-seeing rounds.

The Spanish Steps, brilliant example of baroque art, spill down the slope of the Pincian Hill, linking Rome's Trinità dei Monte church with Piazza di Spagna below. Modern Romans enjoy a moonlit performance of the Rome Opera Orchestra in the Colosseum (*below*). Despite tradition and movies, scholars doubt that the Colosseum ever witnessed a Christian thrown to lions.

Roman Forum (*right*), looking west toward splendor as Rome
grew great. Here Romans gathered to worship or
do business, to pass laws or celebrate triumphs, and men
like Julius Caesar went about planting the roots of
Western civilization. A quiet *aperitivo* on the sidewalk (*below*),
with the mighty Colosseum looming in the background.

152

Florence—birthplace of the Renaissance. Wearing plumes and pantaloons of 1530, a drum corps parades in Piazza della Signoria before Michelangelo's *David* and Bandinelli's *Hercules and Cacus*. The drummers herald a zany football game (25 men on each side), one of three annual contests perpetuating the defiance of Florentines who played a similar game in 1530, while French troops were besieging the city.

154

The Florence shop of Alinari Brothers (*top left*), world-famous, caters to art students and art lovers. The ornate double-columned gates (*bottom left*) lead to Florence's Torre del Gallo castle. Galileo is said to have used the tower for experiments. The Tuscan villa, La Torre di Bellosguardo (*bottom right*), now houses Eversholme International School for Girls.

Florence's famous Lapi restaurant (*right*) in Via del Trebbio. Noted for its excellent food and atmosphere. *Left*, formal 17th century gardens of the ancient Villa La Pietra.

Finest of Florentine landscape architecture is the Boboli Gardens, with long vistas and cool grottoes.

Diners on the terrace of Venice's famous
Royal Danieli Hotel (*left*) overlook the historic Piazzetta.
Across the water is Santa Maria della Salute church.
Below, a gondolier dressed in colors of the family he works
for and wearing the family crest—in this case a stork—
on his silver arm plaque and buttons.

159

Favorite shore-line spot on Capri is villa-strewn beach of Piccola Marina.

Outdoor living, Capri style, is accented by soft colors and sharp sun, ease and opulence. *At right:* the Countess Medina Arrivebene breakfasting on her terrazzo in Anacapri; the painter Novella Parigini gracing the steps of Robert Hornstein's handsome house; (*below left*) Prince Dado Ruspoli in the colorful lounge suit he designed himself. The must thing to do in Capri is to hire a *sandalino* boat (*below right*) and go swimming in the incredibly clear water of one of countless coves.

Wedding-cake balconies and spun-sugar fretwork typify the unique and entirely charming palazzo architecture of Venice. Striped poles and gondola crests (*right*) identify owners.

Amalfi Coast: Cetara, one of the villages on the exquisite Amalfi Drive.

Tuscan Hill Town: Lovely

Paestum: The Temple of Poseidon where the Sybarites, devotees of luxury and pleasure, worshipped.

San Gimignano and its 13 medieval towers.

Rome: The majestic Forum, nerve center of the entire classical world.

Dolomites: A mighty backdrop for a mountain village in the Cadore Valley.

Naples: The Bay, looking to-

Tuscany: Washed wine bottles drying in Certaldo, Boccaccio's home town.

Florence: Ponte Vecchio and

ward Vesuvius across Santa Lucia harbor.

Liguria: Portofino framed by oleanders and busy with pleasure boats.

the Arno River in the middle of a thunderstorm.

Lombardy: The resort of Menaggio, at the widest point of Lake Como.

Siena

Assisi, Church of St. Francis

Perugia

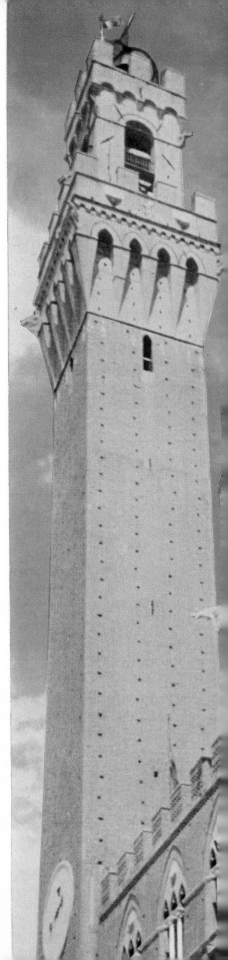

The Golden Hill Towns of
Italy (*left*). Siena's 13th Century
Palazzo Pubblico, or town
hall (*right*), brightens its aged
face with heraldic flags.
Above it, the Mangia Towers,
a striking landmark
since the Middle Ages,
soars boldly into
the skies of Tuscany.

Islands everywhere, from a tiny dot of wooded green in the middle of a lake to a great subcontinent, have always fascinated the wandering mainlander. Tahiti, Bermuda, Hawaii, the Antilles, the East Indies, the Azores—the yearning for them, the urge to visit and explore them is world-wide and irresistible. Of the world's islands, Sicily is one of the liveliest and loveliest. Sicily, just off the toe of the Italian boot, is a midway island—midway between Spain and Turkey, midway between Africa and Europe, the ancient dividing point of an ancient, much-traveled sea. As such, it is more than a crossroads: it is a no man's land and an everyman's land which has been coveted and crossed and conquered by armies and commanders from the very dawn of history, the last time by American troops in World War II. Yet it has never been crushed, not in spirit, not in looks. Sicily today is furiously alive, burning with vigor and activity under a hot, year-round sun. You see this life in the swarms of farmers and fishermen and seamen who make Sicily one of the most crowded spots of land anywhere. It is reflected in the traditional Sicilian passions which produce knives in the dark, folk heroes like the bandit raiders, Guiliano, and vendetta-crime organizations like the Maffia. You see it in the endless and lovely orchards of olives, almonds, oranges, lemons and grapes which make Sicily—dry, hot, rocky Sicily—the greenest and sweetest-smelling spot in the Mediterranean. Everywhere in Sicily this same extraordinary aliveness: in the bright-painted carts of the peasants, in the shouting activity of the great seaports of Messina, Palermo, Catania and Syracuse, in the vigor and success of the tuna and swordfishing fleets. You see it also in Sicily's past—in the vast relics left by Greeks, Romans, Saracens, Spaniards, Italians; in a whole valley of Greek temples at Agrigento and in the incredible artistic riches of Palermo. You find it, too, in Sicily's wonders—the dangers of Scylla and Charybdis, the lure of the fata morgana mirage, the wild destructiveness of volcanic Etna.

But Sicily has its peaceful side too. It is perhaps best experienced at Taormina, the jewel of the island. Here, on a tiny town set on a terrace 500 feet above the sea, one may look to the south, past the remains of a Greek-Roman theater (*left*), at the extraordinary snowy flank and peak of Mount Etna. Here the February air is warm enough to encourage swimming on the fine beaches below, quiet enough to carry the heady whiff of the season's first almond blossoms. Here one may feel, like an earlier traveler named Goethe: ". . . happy to have in my soul such a clear, whole and pure image of the great, beautiful and incomparable Sicily."

Italy's great past and vibrant present merge in the ancient amphitheater— 375 feet in diameter—at Taormina during Carnival (*see page following*).

Portofino, tiny, dazzling, is the new darling of the Italian Riviera, a favorite of movie people and yachtsmen. Fishermen's homes, now luxury flats, retain their gentle colors, and the perfection of the tiny harbor remains the same.

The hoary rock fortress (*above*) is in San Marino, the smallest republic in the world. Occupying thirty-eight square miles in Northern Italy, it is famous for its postage stamps, long cherished by collectors.

The Acropolis, a
squat limestone butte
jutting up a few
hundred feet from
the Attic plain, carries
in its broken ruins
a distillation of
man's groping through
chaos toward reason
and beauty.
In this monument,
in Greece,
civilization was born.

Athena's Temple: The Parthenon from within. This most perfect Greek structure survived for 2125 years in use as temple, church, mosque and Turkish powder magazine, until Venetians shelled and blew it up in 1687.

The lines of the Parthenon look straight but actually curve to compensate for the optical illusion. *Opposite page* is a view of modern Athens, offspring of the city Athena protected long ago.

Marble lions, carved in Roman times, sun themselves on the stairway that leads to the Acropolis.

Temple of Athena Nike, the Wingless Victory.
Marble columns (*opposite page*) flank the main gate
of the Propylaea, grand entrance to
the Athenian citadel in the 5th century B.C.

The living get along companionably
with the past on the Greek islands.
Volcanic Santorini (*above*) thrives near
once-inhabited island bits that casually sink
down or pop up to the surface.
The houses on Mykonos (*right*) gleam
with whitewash sometimes ground
from marble ruins on nearby Delos.

The Palace of Minos at Cnossos, heart of the elegant and intensely pleasure-loving civilization that flowered on Crete while the Greeks were still barbarians.

Before the south wind, *lodos*, gives way to the first tingling blasts of the black wind, *karayel*, the long, incredibly beautiful autumn begins in Istanbul. The air is clear, the sunshine pervading. Its raw gold light gives the domed mosques and minarets a rich, tawny sheen. Galata and Beyoglu, the newer and European sections, are parted from historic Stamboul by that fabled arm of the Bosporus, the Golden Horn, and relinked by busy bridges like the Galata (*see picture*). The whole area has a floating look.

The uplift of autumn is shared by tourist and habitué alike, and the jammed streets of this ancient crossroads between Europe and the Orient show it. Greeks, Armenians, Italians, French, Yugoslavs, Jews and many other Turkish nationals share the city with the Moslem Turks, all 1,179,666 of them preoccupied with progress as expressed by the tumult of shipping in the harbor and the bustling shops of the business districts. Istanbul resembles a movie set for an international spy thriller which in this day of tensions it might well be. Yet tourists looking for the mysteriously wicked Istanbul of the old storybooks will be surprised to find that the Turk of today goes to bed early.

There are, of course, a few spots, such as the Turkish Government's Taksim Kazino (known to Istanbul playboys as "the Snake Pit"), glad to convince customers that foreign liquor comes high. Smarter tourists settle for some truly great Turkish eating at Pandeli's, for instance, a hole-in-the-wall in the market section of old Stamboul, where the fare is epic and the boss, snow-maned Pandeli himself, roars at his waiters in a variety of languages.

There is irony in the rediscovery of Istanbul by the visitor from the West. This city was a going concern in Greek times, six centuries before Christ. As Constantinople, it was the golden heart of the Eastern Roman Empire for a thousand years. When it fell to the Ottoman Turks under Mehmet II, in 1453, it became the cultural and religious pride of the Moslem empire, a place of inspired architects, poets, artists, musicians. Part of a democratic Republic today, Istanbul still cherishes a past manifest in its best-loved sights: St. Sophia (Ayasofya) built as a Christian church by the Roman emperor Justinian, converted into a mosque by the Turks, and later restored and turned into a museum by Ataturk in 1935 ... the Suleymaniye, the most beautiful specimen of Islamic art in Istanbul, the mosque whose antique columns were taken from the old Byzantine hippodrome.

This is a romance city where the smoke of the narghile, the water pipe, bubbles through rose water and the Turkish bath is still a ceremonial institution. It is a city that has a great, innate and soft-spoken politeness to the American within its gates. It's wonderful in the fall.

Sights and sounds of Istanbul:
The 17th-century Mosque of Sultan
Ahmet (*opposite page*, *left*), one of
the very few in all Islam with
six minarets. The towers (*above*) of
Rumelihisari, constructed in 1452
by conqueror Mehmet Fatih, recall
the last days of Constantinople.
In the Blue Mosque (*right*),
260 windows still pour mystic light
into the richly tiled interior.

Kotor lies in a spectacular mountain-girt fiord on Yugoslavia's Dalmatian coast. Many vacationers start their trip north by taking the bus from here to Dubrovnik.

Small yachtlike boats leave from

Dubrovnik (*above*) for the cruise up the Adriatic. The water is deep blue, the shores dotted with colors of subtropical flowers.

The market place in Dubrovnik, one of the most colorful and delightful of all Europe's medieval walled cities. It offers excellent beaches, magnificent scenery and a balmy climate.

PHOTO AND ART CREDITS

PAGE

2-3 David Seymour
6 British Travel Association
7 Air France; Spanish Tourist
   Office; Ente Provinciale
   per il Turismo, Roma
8 Casa de Portugal
9 German Tourist Information
   Office; Royal Greek
   Embassy
10 Austrian State Tourist
   Department; Official
   Belgian Tourist Bureau
17 Studio Graphis—Pix
18-19 Ruth Gray (F.P.G.)
20-21 Tom Hollyman
22-23 Tom Hollyman
   Right—Slim Aarons
24-25 British Travel Association
26-27 Arnold Newman
28-29 Slim Aarons
30-31 Cornell Capa
32-33 Cornell Capa
34-35 British Travel Association
   Right—Slim Aarons
36-37 Slim Aarons
38-39 Slim Aarons
40 Slim Aarons
43 Jean and Tom Hollyman
44-45 George Pickow (Three Lions)
46-47 Jean and Tom Hollyman
48-49 Jean and Tom Hollyman
50 Jean and Tom Hollyman
53 Robert Capa
54 Robert Capa
55 Slim Aarons
56-57 Ewing Krainin
   Right—Erich Lessing
58-59 Ewing Krainin
   Right—Morton D. Spector
60 Erich Lessing
61 Ewing Krainin
62 Robert Capa
65 Josef Muench
66-67 Henri Cartier-Bresson
68-69 Charlotte and Denis Plimmer
70-71 Josef Muench
72 Kryn Taconis
75 Josef Muench
76-77 Duncan Edwards (F.P.G.)
78-79 David Seymour
   Right—Jean Chevalier

PAGE

80-81 David Seymour
82-83 Dennis Stock
84-85 Rene Jacques
   (Rapho-Guillumette)
   Dynevor Rhys (Pix)
86-87 Ewing Krainin
88 J. R. Johnson
   (Rapho-Guillumette)
   Right—Cameron McDermott
   (Black Star)
89 Three Lions
90 Sabine Weiss
   (Rapho-Guillumette)
91 Ace Williams (Shostal)
92-93 Henri Cartier-Bresson
95 Duncan Edwards (F.P.G.)
96-97 Carl Perutz
   Right—A. Pedrett
   (Magnum)
98-99 Carl Perutz
   Right—Don Harris
100-101 Ardean Miller (F.P.G.)
   Right—Josef Muench
102-103 Duncan Edwards (F.P.G.)
104-105 Slim Aarons
106-107 Duncan Edwards (F.P.G.)
108-109 Duncan Edwards (F.P.G.)
110-111 Ewing Krainin
112-113 Ewing Krainin
114 Erich Lessing
115 Henri Cartier-Bresson
116-117 Erich Lessing
118-119 Three Lions
120 Davis Pratt
   (Rapho-Guillumette)
123 Ewing Krainin
124-125 Henri Cartier-Bresson
126-127 Henri Cartier-Bresson
128-129 Henri Cartier-Bresson
130-131 Ewing Krainin
132-133 Ewing Krainin
134-135 Ewing Krainin
   Right—Robert Barclay
   (F.P.G.)
136-137 Norman Parkinson
138-139 Henri Cartier-Bresson
140-141 Ewing Krainin
   Right—Robert Barclay
   (F.P.G.)
142 Ewing Krainin
145 Kryn Taconis

PAGE

146-147 Josef Muench
148-149 Ewing Krainin
   Right—Robert Capa
150-151 Ewing Krainin
   Right—Robert Capa
152-153 Ewing Krainin
154-155 Herbert Kratovil
156-157 Ewing Krainin
158-159 Ewing Krainin
   Right—Arnold Newman
160-161 Arnold Newman
162-163 Top left—Slim Aarons
   Bottom left—J. D. Barnell
   (Shostal)
   Bottom center—Duncan
   Edwards (F.P.G.)
   Two at right—
   Arnold Newman
164-165 Top left and lower right—
   Duncan Edwards
   (F.P.G.)
   Top center—
   Arnold Newman
   Top right—Slim Aarons
   Bottom left—
   Henri Cartier-Bresson
   (Magnum)
   Bottom Center—
   Alexander Wainman
166-167 Top left and right
   Charles J. Belden
   Left center—Duncan
   Edwards (F.P.G.)
   Bottom left—J. D. Barnell
168-169 J. D. Barnell
170-171 Duncan Edwards (F.P.G.)
172 Duncan Edwards (F.P.G.)
173 J. D. Barnell (Shostal)
174-175 Duncan Edwards (F.P.G.)
176-177 Bob Garland
178-179 Bob Garland
180-181 Rathenan (Pix)
   Right—Louis
   and Melissa Levi
182-183 Erich Lessing
184-185 Ewing Krainin
186-187 Duncan Edwards (F.P.G.)
   Right—Three Lions
188-189 Bakal (Pix)
   Right—Fred Maroon
190 Bakal (Pix)

INDEX

Acropolis, Greece . . 174, 175, 178
Alcazar, Spain 138, 139
Amalfi, Italy 162
Anacapri, Italy 161
Arcos de la Frontera,
    Spain 130, 131
Ascot, England 37, 40
Assisi, Italy 166
Athens, Greece 176, 177
AUSTRIA 115-120
Ávila, Spain 132, 133
Barrington, England 31
Bavaria, Germany . . . 110, 111
BELGIUM 68, 69
Berlin, Germany 114
Bibury, England 32
Blue Mosque, Istanbul . . . 187
Bourton-on-the-Water,
    England 31
Bruges, Belgium 68, 69
Bürgenstock, Switzerland . 104, 105
Cadore Valley, Italy 164
CAPRI 160, 161
Cassis, France 93
Certaldo, Italy 164
Cetara, Italy 162
Chantilly, France 81
Chartres Cathedral,
    France 88, 89
Château Chambord,
    France 90
Château d'If, France 92
Claridge's Hotel, London . . . 28
Cnossus, Crete 182, 183
Colosseum, Rome 151
Córdoba, Spain 137
Cork, Ireland 48
Cotswold, England 30-33
CRETE 182, 183
DENMARK 56-61
Dublin, Ireland 48, 49
Dubrovnik, Yugoslavia . . 189, 190
Dürnstein, Austria 117
Edinburgh, Duke of 35
ENGLAND 17-40
Fano, Denmark 57
Florence, Italy . . 154-157, 164, 165
Folies Bergère, Paris 82
FRANCE 75-93
Frogner Park, Oslo 54
Fünen, Denmark 60
GERMANY 110-114
Glen of Two Lakes, Ireland . . 45
Gouda, Holland 67
Granada, Spain 140, 141

GREECE 174-183
Grindelwald, Switzerland . . . 95
Gross Glockner, Austria . 118, 119
Hammerfest, Norway 53
Heiligenblut, Austria . . . 116
Henley, England 37-39
HOLLAND . . . 65-67, 72
House of Commons,
    England 26
House of Lords, England . . 27
Howth Castle, Ireland . . . 49
Innsbruck, Austria 117
IRELAND 43-50
Istanbul, Turkey 184-187
ITALY 146-172
Jungfrau, Switzerland . . 108, 109
Kaiser Wilhelm Memorial
    Church, Berlin 114
Kerry, Ireland 50
Kleine Scheidegg,
    Switzerland 108, 109
Kotor, Yugoslavia 188
Lapps, Norway 54, 62
Lech am Arlberg, Austria . . 120
Leitrim, Ireland 47
Liffey River, Ireland 48
Liguria, Italy 165
Limerick, Ireland 46
Little Rissington, England . . 33
Loire Valley, France . . . 86, 87
Lombardy, Italy 165
London, England . . . 17, 20-29
Lord's, London 36
Lough Allen, Ireland 47
Louvre, Paris 2-3
LUXEMBOURG 70-71
Madrid, Spain 134, 140
Maggiore, Italy 146, 147
Marseilles, France 92
Matterhorn, Switzerland . 100, 101
Menaggio, Italy 165
MONACO 145
Monte Carlo, Monaco . . . 145
Montmartre, France 78
Mont-Saint-Michel, France . . 75
Moselle Valley, Germany . 112, 113
Mykonos, Greece . . . 180, 181
Naples, Italy 164, 165
Nazaré, Portugal 127
Neuschwanstein Castle,
    Germany 110, 111
Normandy, France 91
NORWAY 53, 54, 62
Nyhavn, Denmark 58
Obidos, Portugal 123

O'Connell Street Bridge,
    Dublin 48
Odense, Denmark 60
Oslo, Norway 54
Paestum, Italy 163
Palma, Mallorca 142
Paris, France 76-83
Parthenon, Greece 176
Perugia, Italy 166
Ponte Vecchio, Florence . . . 164
Portofino, Italy 165, 172
PORTUGAL 123-129
Ribe, Denmark 59
Ritz Gardens, Paris 81
Rock of Cashel, Ireland . . . 43
Rome, Italy 148-153, 163
Royal Palace, Sweden 55
Sacré-Coeur, Paris 78
St. James Park, London . . . 23
St. Moritz, Switzerland . . . 96-99
St. Wolfgang, Austria . . . 116
Salzburg, Austria 115
San Gimignano, Italy . . . 163
SAN MARINO 173
Santorini, Greece 180
SCANDINAVIA 53-62
Seville, Spain 135, 136
SICILY 168-171
Siena, Italy 166, 167
SPAIN 130-141
Spanish Steps, Rome 150
Spree River, Germany 114
Steffani Hotel, St. Moritz . . . 96
Stockholm, Sweden 55
SWEDEN 55
SWITZERLAND 94-109
Taormina, Sicily 168-171
Thun Lake, Switzerland . 106, 107
Tipperary, Ireland 43
Tivoli Gardens, Denmark . . . 56
Torquay, England 34
Tower of London 20
Traun Lake, Austria 116
Trooping of the Colours,
    England 24, 25
TURKEY 184-187
Tuscany, Italy 163, 164
Venice, Italy . . . 158, 159, 162
Versailles, France 84, 85
Viana do Castelo, Portugal . . 126
Volendam, Holland 72
White Tower, London 29
YUGOSLAVIA 188-190
Zermatt, Switzerland . . . 100, 101
Zurich, Switzerland . . . 102, 103